ECHOES
ECHOING CHRIST

Parish-based training for handing on Faith

Participants' Book

CONTENTS

Welcome
to this **parish** and
family resource!

HAVE YOU ever felt that you wanted to pass on your Faith to others but were uncertain how to go about it?

HAVE YOU been asked to help out in a parish with preparation for one of the sacraments, or as a member of the parish RCIA team?

AS A PARENT, have you wished you were able to share the Faith with your children more easily?

WOULD YOU LIKE TO KNOW MORE ABOUT YOUR FAITH so you can speak with others about it, at work, in the home or the parish?

IF SO, THEN THIS RESOURCE IS DESIGNED TO HELP YOU!
The Church's mission is to to hand on the Faith to others. This is a responsibility and a privilege in which we can all share. We hope and pray that this resource will lead you to appreciate even more the treasure of the Faith, to experience the love and grace of God which flows to us through the wisdom of the Church, and will equip you to participate in handing on Christ in his Church to others.

Sessions

Session 1 What is the Good News?
'The Truth will make you free' (John 8:32)   Date:

Session 2 Why the Holy Spirit?
'The Holy Spirit, whom the Father will send in my name,
he will teach you all things, and bring to your remembrance
all that I have said to you.' (John 14:26)   Date:

Session 3 Why the Church?
'He who hears you, hears me' (Luke 10:16)   Date:

Session 4 Why the Catechism?
'Father... this is eternal life, that they may know You' (John 17:3)   Date:

Session 5 Who teaches?
'As the Father sent me so I send you' (John 20:21)   Date:

Session 6 Whose Story?
'He interpreted for them all the scriptures' (Luke 24:27)   Date:

Session 7 Who are we?
'You shall be consecrated to me' (Exodus 22:31)   Date:

Session 8 Why link with the liturgy?
'Christ, our spiritual and eternal sacrifice' (Cf. Hebrews 9:14)   Date:

Session 9 What is the Mystery?
'Worship the Father in Spirit and in Truth' (John 4:23)   Date:

Session 10 What can we do?
'Do whatever he tells you' (John 2:5)   Date:

Session 11 What next?
'Put out into the deep' (Luke 5:4)   Date:

Venue: Date:

Session 1

What is the Good News?

'The truth will make you free' (Jn 8:32)

*Loving God,
Pour out your Spirit on this parish and grant us a new vision of your glory, a new experience of your power, a new faithfulness to your Word, and a new consecration to your service that your love may grow among us, and your Kingdom come. Amen*

We begin this session by exploring what we mean by the 'Good News' that Christ came to bring. We seek to understand this Good News so that we can pass it on to others.

We then go on to look at the meaning of the title of the course, 'Echoes, Echoing Christ' as a way of understanding who we are as Catholics and what it means to pass on, or 'echo on' the faith of the Church.

Good News

The world in which we wake and live each day appears to us as a puzzle. It is a place of pain, and also of deep happiness. We experience periods of satisfaction, but all too often these are unstable or the satisfaction turns to boredom. We know the promise that love brings but also the numbness that comes with the loss of love or a loved one. The world is a place bright with beauty and hope, but at the same time is filled with dark shadows of injustice, evil and death in which thousands die each day from malnutrition and millions live in loneliness.

The Christian stands in this world able to speak the pure, life-giving words of the Gospel. 'Gospel' means 'Good News'. The Old English word 'gospel' comes from the Anglo Saxon 'godspell' meaning 'good speech or message'. It directly translates the Greek word *'evangelion'* meaning 'Good News'. The Christian can speak this Good News with certainty because it comes with the authority of the God who created the universe and holds it in his hands day by day.

The world has need of this Good News, although it is not always welcome. For like a doctor examining a wound in order to cleanse and heal it, God reveals to us our true condition so that we can seek the only treatment for our healing.

The Diagnosis

The diagnosis: we live in a state of fatal disharmony. The four essential relationships in our lives have received a death-wound. Each of us is in relation with

- God our Creator and Father
- other human beings
- the earth that is our dwelling-place
- our own self that should be a harmonious unity of body, emotions, mind, will and spirit.

The first chapters of the Bible vividly describe the breakdown in these relationships, as disharmony and conflict replace the happiness and stability God seeks for our lives.

The root problem is the mistrust and fear of our very source of life, God the Father, who wants only good for his children. The human person is frightened of a distorted image of the Father who, he thinks, gives him commands and orders obedience, but does not give him what he needs for his happiness. What he thinks God will not give, man then seeks to take for himself. He shuts God out and even treats eternal Love as an enemy.

But cut off from true Life, the human person is like a branch that withers from lack of sap running through it. What he hopes will be a garden of his own making often becomes only a wilderness. Love and true happiness seem to evade so many who are around us. Life is distorted and even destroyed in a vain attempt to secure a good future. Other human beings, the earth, one's bodily life, are ransacked in the search for a final happiness they can never give. When this happens, those around us are used rather than loved, the earth is exploited, the body scarred.

The inner conflict that we all find in ourselves is summed up well by St. Paul in his *Letter to the Romans* 7:14-28.

1 **Look at the passage from Romans Chapter 7 on the handout.**

- **Quietly reflect on the following prayer of the Church: 'Lord, guide us in your gentle mercy, for left to ourselves we cannot do your will.' (Roman Missal, Mass of the Saturday of the Fourth Week of Lent, Opening Prayer).**

The world is in need of healing from all disharmony and distorted relationships.

The Remedy

God reveals our state of sin and ruin to us only gradually. When he comes Jesus says, 'I have many things to say to you, but you cannot bear them now' (Jn 16:12). He lets us see our true condition only as he reveals his plan of loving-kindness, his plan to rescue us. It is not easy to welcome his rescue because it is not easy to face the reality of what our lives become without God. But as our eyes are opened to the immensity of God the Father's love we can gradually accept the truth about ourselves.

To demonstrate his love, the Father sent his Son among us, to lift us out of the pit into which we had fallen. He came to mend our wounded state, to heal our broken relationships and to unite us to the only Source of true life, his Son.

The name given to the remedy is 'redemption', and the simple means by which this is given is 'Baptism', an immersion in water that is made in the name of the Father who made us, the Son who redeems us and the Spirit who guides us into all truth as he renews us.

To live this life of gradual healing in God, we take up our Cross to follow Jesus Christ, who called himself the Way, the Truth, and the Life (Jn 14:6).

Because of the ongoing effects of the state from which we are rescued in Baptism, the state that the Church calls 'original sin', our actions and motives are not automatically good and pure. It is like trying to drive straight with a flat front tyre - you are pulled off the centre of the road, and keeping on course needs a sustained pull on the steering wheel. So it is with our life in Christ: it means holding one's gaze fixed on Christ who is our hope and relying on his grace at every moment.

The Good News is that God the loving Father does not leave us on our own. He sends his Holy Spirit who strengthens us to live in Christ more and more fully. God freely pours out his grace upon us, pours out his own life, to transform each of us into the image of Jesus Christ. 'Grace is everything God grants us, without our deserving it in the least.' (YOUCAT 338).

This is the Good News that each Christian has to share. Not just a message but a new life. Not just a more satisfying life, but the promise of deep joy. This is what we are called to pass on to others. And the name given to the handing on of the Good News is 'catechesis'.

2 **Look up the Gospel account on the Handout of the healing of Peter's mother-in-law by Jesus in Matthew 8:14-15.**

- **Look at the actions of Jesus and of Peter's mother-in-law. What does this tell us about God's work and about our needs and our response to God?**

God has sent his Son and Spirit among us to rescue and heal us.

Catechesis

'Catechesis' is an unfamiliar word to most of us. It comes from the Greek word *'catechein'*, originally meaning 'to echo'. In the time of St. Paul it was used to mean 'to hear', 'to learn', or 'to instruct'.

Catechesis, then, is about hearing, learning and teaching. And this teaching and learning can be thought of as a kind of echoing. An echo is like a reflection. When we look at a reflection in a mirror we know that what we are looking at is a picture, an image, and not the whole of the reality itself.

A catechist is like a mirror. Those who are learning from a catechist are catching glimpses of a Figure, they are hearing echoes of a Voice who is calling to them and drawing them to Himself through the words and life of the catechist.

The glossary at the end of this session explains the variety of words associated with 'catechesis'.

Echoing a message

Catechesis, then, is the 'echoing' or 'resounding' of a message. It is handing on what has been received. That is what St Paul meant when he said that 'I handed on to you that which was handed on to me' (1 Cor 15:3). St Paul has received the message and now he is 'echoing' it on to others. To be a catechist is to receive and to hand on what has been received.

Catechists hand on a precious message, the Good News. Nothing is more valuable than this, nothing is more important; it is the pearl of great price about which Jesus spoke in the Gospels. It is the News which every person needs to hear.

A catechist, therefore, is one who, realising 'the riches of grace' (Ephesians 1:7) which have been poured out on the world through Christ, is willing to spend time learning about this message of Good News and learning how to teach it so that it may be faithfully and accurately 'echoed' to others.

Scripture calls this precious message a 'Deposit' because it has been entrusted by God to his Church: 'Guard the deposit which has been entrusted to you.' (1 Timothy 6:20). The 'deposit', the riches of Christ's message, have been entrusted to the Church and we all receive this from the Church. We receive it from the Church whose members have, down through the centuries, guarded it, celebrated it, lived it, been nourished by it, and died for it.

Catechesis is an echoing or transmission of a message which the catechist receives from the Church.

Echoing a Person

What we echo is more than just a precious message. We echo a Person. We are not only learning a series of truths and helping others to learn these. We are not only learning *about* Christ. We want to 'gain Christ and be found in Him' (Philippians 3:8-9) and to help others to know and experience the depths of His love. We are opening ourselves, then, to listen not just to a message but to the voice of a Person, the divine Person of Jesus Christ. We are learning to echo Him. In our being with others we are asking others to listen to Him.

The Church teaches that God has said all that He wants to say by sending Christ. Jesus is the Word of God. He is the perfect revelation of God and of His plan of love and salvation. The Father has only one thing He wants to say: 'Listen to my beloved Son, listen to my Word'.

Catechesis is concerned with teaching the faith in order to open the heart to conversion, so that those whom we teach may hear and receive Christ, the Word.

Catechists echo not just a message but a Person.

Summary

In this first session we have been looking at:

- **What is the Good News that we bring.**
- **Our fallen state and how we have been rescued.**
- **What a catechist is.**
- **The catechist as one who echoes both a message and a Person.**

Further reading

- On our original state and the Fall after our first sin: Genesis Chs 1-3; CCC 374, 379; CCC 385-388. *(CCC 374 means Catechism of the Catholic Church, paragraph 374)*

- On the Incarnation of the Son of God: Jn 1:1-18; CCC 456-460.

- On the meaning of the word 'catechesis': CCC 4.

- On proclaiming Christ: CCC 74.

Glossary

Meanings of words associated with catechesis
Catechist: *the **person** communicating the message*
Catechesis: the ***action*** of communicating the message
Catechism: a book of the ***content*** of the message to be communicated
Catechumen: ***a receiver*** of what is communicated in preparation for Baptism
Catechumenate: the ***period*** of instruction to catechumens
Catechetics: ***guidelines*** for communicating

Final meditation and prayer

God has created me to do him some definite service. He has committed some work to me which He has not committed to another.
(John Henry Newman)

Father, let the gift of your life continue to grow in us drawing us from death to faith, hope and love. Keep us alive in Christ Jesus.
Keep us watchful in prayer and true to his teaching till your glory is revealed in us. Amen.
(Roman Missal: Mass of the 16th Sunday in Ordinary Time, Alternative Opening Prayer)

Session 2

Why the Holy Spirit?

'The Holy Spirit, whom the Father will send in my name, he will teach you all things, and bring to your remembrance all that I have said to you.' (Jn 14:26)

Come Holy Spirit, Creator come, from thy bright heavenly throne. Come take possession of our souls and make them all thine own. O guide our minds with thy blest light, with love our hearts inflame, and with your strength which never decays confirm our mortal frame. Amen

In session one we deepened our understanding of Jesus Christ as 'Good News'. Jesus is Good News because he is the Redeemer of the world. Our world is damaged, wounded and needs healing. This session explores how the Holy Spirit works in the Church to make this Good News known to the world.

Three key terms are introduced in this session: Tradition, Scripture and Magisterium. The Holy Spirit hands on Christ in and through the Church's Living Tradition and her Scriptures, and the voice of Christ also speaks to the world today through her Magisterium. Let us see what this means.

Pentecost

First, let us remember Pentecost. Let us remember what happened fifty days after the Resurrection of Jesus from the dead. Look again at the Scripture passage from John's Gospel at the beginning of this session.

Notice that the three persons of the Trinity are all mentioned. The apostles gathered in an upper room; Jesus' promise came true; the apostles were filled with the Holy Spirit; it was the moment the Church was born.

John's Gospel tells us many things to answer the question 'Why the Holy Spirit?' - that is, why the Apostles needed the Holy Spirit, and what the Holy Spirit would do for them. Already in the quotation for this session we see that the Holy Spirit will *'teach them* all things' and will *'bring to their remembrance'* all that Christ had said to them. In another passage John tells us that the Holy Spirit will *'guide them* into all the truth' (Jn 16:13).

The Holy Spirit is the sure teacher, reminder and guide for the Apostles as they lead Christ's disciples in the early Church.

Handing on Christ

The Church 'hands on' Christ. In the Gospel of Matthew Jesus explains to his disciples what this means when he says,

'Go therefore and make disciples of all nations, baptising them in the name of the Father, and of the Son and of the Holy Spirit, teaching them to observe all that I have commanded you' (Matt 28:19-20).

'Handing on' Christ, then, means going to people and telling them about Jesus Christ so that they can be disciples (a word which means 'followers'). Jesus' disciples are those who listen and learn from him and who go where he goes, who think as he thinks, who love what he loves and who pray to him. The Church also 'hands on' Christ when she baptises and when she celebrates the other sacraments. And she teaches her members how to live in Christ by 'observing' all that he 'commanded' and taught.

The Latin for 'handing on' or 'handing over' is 'Traditio', from which we get the word **Tradition**. Notice that Tradition, the handing on of Christ, was taking place before anything was written down in the New Testament and has continued everyday wherever the Church lives. It is the work of the Holy Spirit in the Church. It includes the teaching of the apostles, celebrating the sacraments, praying and living in Christ.

Magisterium

The apostles appointed successors to continue to their work, called 'bishops' (which means 'overseers'). The successors of the Apostles are the 'masters' or 'master teachers' of the Truth and of what Jesus truly said, and they are guided continually by the Holy Spirit. The Latin word for 'master' is *magister*, from which we derive the word **Magisterium**. The bishops in union with the successor of Peter, the bishop of Rome, are the magisterium and we can trust that the Holy Spirit keeps his promises to them. Reading the writings of the magisterium, then, is a way of knowing with certainty that the words of Jesus are being remembered and interpreted truly for us today.

In the Tradition of the Church guided by the Magisterium we meet the living body of Christ. In this way, the Holy Spirit hands on Christ, from generation to generation.

The Bible

Where does the Bible fit in? The churches founded by the apostles were teaching, listening, believing, baptising, celebrating the Eucharist, and living Christian lives for many years before any writings about Christ were gathered together into what we now know as the New Testament.

The first Christians were also reflecting deeply upon God's deeds and promises in the Old Testament, rejoicing in all that had now been fulfilled in Christ. They knew that these Scriptures were written under the inspiration of the Holy Spirit and have God as their divine author. This is why the Catechism of the Catholic Church says about both the Old and New Testaments:

'Through all the words of Sacred Scripture, God speaks only one single Word, his one utterance in whom he expresses himself completely' (CCC 102).

When the authors of the four Gospels began to preserve in writing the truth of what Jesus said and did, who he was and what happened to him, they were able to include how the Old Testament also spoke of Christ as the One who fulfilled the promises of God.

❶ Look at the structure and contents of the New Testament. Notice the letters and who they are from. Then identify the four Gospels, then the Acts of the Apostles, then finally the Book of Revelation.

The Bible is a single book and at the same time a library. It is made up of different writings born over a thousand year period. The writings tell of many different figures, they have different human authors, they are written in a variety of literary styles and they have emerged from different historical contexts. But there is a single God revealing Himself through them, and they tell of a single plan of salvation that unfolds in history. Moreover, the writings are directed to a single People of God. And, finally, they have a common centre in Christ. Every page of the Scriptures can be properly understood only in the light of this single plan of salvation and by reference to Christ.

Note on finding Bible references

The Bible is divided into books, chapters and verses. A Bible reference tells us which book, chapter and verse we should go to in order to find the lines we want. The books of the Bible are given in abbreviated form. So, for example 'Rom 1:20' means St Paul's Letter to the Romans, Chapter 1 and verse twenty.

❷ Let us look at some verses from the New Testament. Find and read the following portions from the Scriptures and see whether you can identify any of the three elements of Tradition, Magisterium and Scripture.
- **Matthew 28:18-20**
- **Acts of the Apostles 2:42**
- **1 Corinthians 15:1-4**
- **2 Thessalonians 2:15**
- **2 Timothy 3:14-17**
- **Titus 1:7-9**

When we want to hand on Christ we need to be nourished by the Scriptures.

Already from the New Testament writers of the early Church one can identify the living message of salvation which was being carefully taught, received, delivered, held and passed on.

God reveals Himself and His single plan of salvation to us in Scripture and Tradition. These are the living wells from which we drink so as to be able to quench our own and others' thirst for the living Lord.

We look to Scripture and Tradition, guided by the Holy Spirit promised to the Magisterium, in order to receive and hand on the true life and message of Jesus Christ.

The Catechism of the Catholic Church

The Catechism of the Catholic Church is a wonderful example of Scripture and Tradition gathered together by the Magisterium for our day. It was finalised in 1997, and is a completely up-to-date account of the Catholic faith. Every Catholic adult should have a copy on his or her bookshelf. We can turn to this reference work when we would like to know and understand the teaching of the Church on any subject.

We conclude today's session by looking at the introduction to the Catechism, written by Blessed Pope John Paul II. This introduction is called *'Fidei Depositum'*, the Deposit of Faith. This is a phrase used by St Paul for the 'treasure' that has been given, or 'deposited' for safe keeping for all generations, to the Church by God the Father. The treasure is God the Son and the Holy Spirit, who are the treasure of the truth about life and happiness. This is the treasure of the faith of the Church.

Catechism

1. Read the opening two paragraphs of *'Fidei Depositum'* and find:

   • how the mission of the Church is described.

   • the task given to the Second Vatican Council by Pope John XXIII,

   • how the Council set out to achieve this task.

2. Read the paragraphs down to the next main heading.

   • What happened 20 years after the Council? What was requested?

3. Notice that the Catechism will provide renewal through connecting its readers to 'the living sources of the faith'. The texts cited in the Catechism are the sources – made 'living' by the Holy Spirit and from which the writers drew inspiration.

   • What are these living sources at the core of the 'deposit of faith'? Check for yourself the index of citations at the back of the Catechism. There you will find Scripture and Tradition.

What did you find when you investigated the index of citations at the end of the Catechism?

Did you see that Scripture is placed first and counts for over half of the whole index? That shows us the vital role that the Scriptures play in providing the foundations for the Church's catechetical work. Then did you see the Creeds, the professions of faith, together with documents from the Church's Councils down through the centuries? Then there were papal writings, references to the law of the Church and to the liturgy, and then to the writings of the Fathers and saints of the Church.

In his introduction to the Catechism the Pope describes this as similar to listening to a great 'symphony' of voices. In the Catechism we hear the voices of the Church down through the centuries coming together in a tremendously inspiring and uplifting harmony. This is the harmony which we as Catholics are called to echo by our lives.

Summary

In this session we have been looking at:

- **The origin of the Church at Pentecost.**

- **The passing on of Christ's life in Scripture and Tradition, guided and protected by the Magisterium.**

- **The Catechism of the Catholic Church as a wonderful example of Scripture, Tradition and magisterium together.**

Further reading

If you have time before the next session you might also like to read the rest of 'Fidei Depositum'.

Final prayer

Come, Holy Spirit, come!
And from your celestial home
Shed a ray of light divine!

You, of comforters the best;
You, the soul's most welcome guest;
Sweet refreshment here below;

In our labour, rest most sweet;
Grateful coolness in the heat;
Solace in the midst of woe.

O most blessed Light divine,
Shine within these hearts of yours,
And our inmost being fill!

Heal our wounds, our strength renew;
On our dryness pour your dew;
Wash the stains of guilt away:

Bend the stubborn heart and will;
Melt the frozen, warm the chill;
Guide the steps that go astray.

On the faithful, who adore
And confess you, evermore
In your sevenfold gift descend:

Give them virtue's sure reward;
Give them your salvation, Lord;
Give them joys that never end.

Session 3

Why the Church?

'He who hears you, hears me'
(Lk 10:16)

*Lord God, renew your
Church with the Spirit of
Wisdom and Love which
you gave so fully to all
the great teachers
of your Church.
Lead us by that same
Spirit to seek you,
the only fountain of true
wisdom and the source of
everlasting love.
We ask this in the name of
Jesus your Son, who lives and
reigns with you and the
Holy Spirit, world without end.
Amen*

**In our last session we considered the
way in which Christ is handed down
to us in Scripture and Tradition.**

**In this session our focus is upon the Church
as our mother and teacher. The teaching
authority of the Church, the Magisterium,
interprets Scripture and Tradition for us
and speaks to us in the name of Christ. In
this session we take time to explore this
in more detail from the Second Vatican
Council and the letters and writings of
the Popes and Congregations in Rome.**

The great grace of the Council

What a treasure there is, dear brothers and sisters, in the
guidelines offered to us by the Second Vatican Council!
...With the passing of the years, the Council documents
have lost nothing of their value or brilliance. They need to
be read correctly, to be widely known and taken to heart
as important and normative texts of the Magisterium,
within the Church's Tradition. Now that the Jubilee has
ended, I feel more than ever in duty bound to point to the
Council as the great grace bestowed on the Church in
the twentieth century: there we find a sure compass by
which to take our bearings in the century now beginning.'

*(Blessed Pope John Paul II, Novo millennio ineunte,
At the Beginning of the New Millennium, 57)*

Church Councils

What is the Second Vatican Council? In order to answer
this question we need to understand what a Council is;
and for this we need to go right back to the beginnings of
the Church. We find the first Church Council recorded
in the Acts of the Apostles as the beginnings of a system
of decision-making. Major doctrinal, liturgical or moral
problems were brought to a gathering of the Apostles
and elders of the Christian communities. The problem
was discussed, the situation was clarified, the truth
was agreed and a decision was made. This was then
communicated by letter to the Christian communities.

You can see this process described in Acts 15. In this
chapter we have recorded for us the first of what have
since been called ecumenical Councils. In two thousand
years there have only been twenty-one such Councils,
each named after the town in which it was held. The
first is usually referred to as the Council of Jerusalem.

1 **Read the story of the first Council in Acts 15:1-35.
You will see distinct stages in the way this Council
proceeds, and it is worth noting**

- **How and where the Apostles and elders met together (vv 2, 6)**
- **What the problem is which needs to be resolved (vv 1,5 & 25)**
- **The discussion of the problem and
resolution of the problem (vv 6-22)**
- **How the decision is communicated to the Christian
communities (vv 22-32)**

From the earliest times Church Councils have been held in order to resolve difficulties and to clarify the teaching of the Church on important matters. The records of their decisions have been handed down to us.

The Second Vatican Council

Now that we have looked at the role of Councils in the Church, let us consider the Second Vatican Council. This was the second Council to have been held at the Vatican, and it is therefore called the Second Vatican Council. Since this Council took place relatively recently – 1962-1965 – it is important that we learn more of what the Spirit has been saying to the Church of our time.

At this Council as many bishops as possible from the whole Church came together to confirm and clarify the faith that has come down to us from the Apostles. Never before have so many bishops from so many different continents and countries been able to gather together. So there never has been such a universal, ecumenical Council before.

Four key documents were drawn up by the Council. They are called 'Constitutions' to distinguish them from the many other documents that were produced. Like political constitutions, these set out fundamental principles about the life of Christ in the Church. The four are:

- The Constitution on the Sacred Liturgy (*Sacrosanctum concilium*)
- The Dogmatic Constitution on the Church (*Lumen gentium*)
- The Constitution on Divine Revelation (*Dei Verbum*)
- The Pastoral Constitution on the Church in the Modern World (*Gaudium et spes*)

Each of these documents has already been the occasion of a significant interior renewal in the Church. But the most profound renewal of the inner life of the Church can only be the result of a deep and spiritual taking to heart of the content of these documents.

Do not be alarmed at the Latin titles. It is the tradition of the Church to keep the official texts in Latin, not just for historical reasons but because Latin allows for exceptional clarity and precision. The first few words of the documents are taken as the title, and are normally deliberately chosen to indicate the key message or content of the text.

4 **Look up the four 'Constitutions' mentioned above, and see this for yourself.**

Then look back at what Blessed Pope John Paul said on the first page of the study sheet about the need to read the documents of Vatican II.

The most significant Council for us to come to know and love is the Second Vatican Council. Here the Spirit is speaking to us in our age through the Church.

Letters

The stages of the Council of Jerusalem that we noted above remain key elements in the Church's decision-making process. The Church today continues to teach us so that we can receive the Faith in a manner similar to that which we discovered when we read Acts chapter 15.

We have already seen that, following the Council of Jerusalem, other great Councils have been held throughout the history of the Church. Other features which we identified in the case of the Council of Jerusalem and which have remained constant are:

- **Letters**. Decisions of the Apostles continue to be communicated by letter. These letters are often called 'Apostolic Exhortation', 'Apostolic Letter' or simply 'Encyclical' (the Latin word for a circular 'letter').

- **The Scriptures.** At the Council of Jerusalem the Apostles were trying to discern what God had been saying to them through the Scriptures and in the life of the People of God. When you read Church documents and letters, you will notice how they also constantly refer to the Scriptures. When she teaches us, the Church draws her inspiration from this living source. Blessed Pope John Paul II, for example, usually begins his letters with a reflection upon a passage of Scripture. For example, the Apostolic Letter, *Novo millennio ineunte,* which we quoted at the beginning of this session, starts with a reference to the 'miraculous catch of fish' (Lk 5:4-6) and the Letter then weaves this theme throughout.

- **Tradition.** There is a tremendous reverence for Tradition in all of the Church's teaching. Church documents refer to previous knowledge in which the leaders of the Church have already come to one accord 'decided unanimously' (Acts 15:25). In most other subject areas, the knowledge of a hundred years ago has been superseded by later discoveries. Knowledge of the Faith is not like this. The Holy Spirit leads the Church into a deeper and broader understanding of God's Revelation given in Christ, but later centuries do not add anything onto the original Deposit of Faith as though the original Revelation was somehow incomplete. Hence, there is a respect, even reverence, shown at the beginning of many documents towards previous Church documents and gatherings because of the recognition that in them we find the unfolding of Tradition and the promised guidance of the Holy Spirit. In the Church, then, no document stands alone or contains an idea completely 'out of the blue'. It will always be in union with the body of truth built upon the teaching of the Apostles and deepened over the centuries. Again, we are aware of echoes, echoing Christ through time by the power of the Holy

- Spirit. It can be awe-inspiring to see the range of references being made in a document, spanning continents and centuries, and demonstrating the unity of the Catholic faith. In the last session you looked at the Catechism of the Catholic Church which is an extraordinary example of this.

5 Following the same process there have been many issues raised about catechesis. These have been discussed at length in Rome and agreement reached and five very important post-conciliar documents (that is, since the Second Vatican Council) have been written:

- The General Catechetical Directory (1971)
- *Evangelii nuntiandi* (Evangelisation in the Modern World) (1975)
- *Catechesi tradendae* (Catechesis in our Time) (1982)
- The Catechism of the Catholic Church (1992)
- The General Directory for Catechesis (1997)

We receive Christ and his Good News through letters written by the successors to the Apostles. These letters manifest a striking reverence for Scripture and Tradition, the sources of God's revelation.

Our Lady

We have focussed to some extent on the beginnings of Church documents. But we also have much to learn from the conclusions to Blessed Pope John Paul II's letters. At the end of each we find references to Our Lady.

The Second Vatican Council decided to include teaching about Our Lady in the Dogmatic Constitution on the Church, in the final chapter, which was called 'The Blessed Virgin Mary, Mother of God, in the mystery of Christ and the Church'. This reminds us that teaching about the Church is incomplete if it does not include Our Lady in her rightful place. The title of that chapter tells us that what the Catholic Faith believes about Mary is based on what it believes about Christ and about the Church, and what it teaches about Mary illumines in turn faith in both Christ and the Church. The way Blessed Pope John Paul II concludes all his teaching with reference to *her* reminds us of the balance we also need to keep in our teaching.

Why is there this close connection between Our Lady, Christ and the Church, so close that we cannot separate them? It is because Mary conceived by the Holy Spirit in her life, and Scripture tells us that she 'pondered' the mystery of Christ in her heart (Lk 2:19). In this keeping of the mystery of Christ in her heart she represents the Church which ponders the mystery over the centuries in order to bring Christ into the lives of each new generation. Thus Mary understands how very much we need the Spirit's divine enlightenment and transforming power as we participate in the Church's teaching ministry, united to the Apostles and their successors.

As catechists we commit ourselves into Mary's care. She is the Mother of Christ and the Church and our mother, too.

To conclude

Now, finally, look at one, or a range, of letters from the pen of Blessed Pope John Paul II and use these to identify a number of the features we have been considering.

6 **In this letter or range of letters from Blessed Pope John Paul II, note:**

- **The kind of document that it is**
- **The Latin title and its meaning**
- **What the document is about**
- **The use of Scripture and the choice of the passages of Scripture**
- **The reverence for Tradition shown in introductory paragraphs and in footnotes**
- **The concluding reference to Our Lady**

Summary

In this third session we have been looking at:

- **The Second Vatican Council.**
- **Some characteristics of Church teaching documents.**
- **The Church as our teacher and our Mother and Our Lady's role in helping us to see this.**
- **Reasons why it is important to be familiar with Church documents.**

Further reading

- For the ways in which Christ is passed down to us in Scripture and Tradition: CCC 688.
- On the role of the Magisterium: CCC 888-892.
- On Our Lady and her significance: CCC 963-970.

Glossary on Councils and documents

Council: *a gathering of the bishops of the Church. The bishops are the successors of the Apostles and have been entrusted with guarding the deposit of faith, the teaching passed down by Christ to the Apostles. In Church Councils the bishops clarify and agree the meaning of aspects of the deposit of faith.*

Ecumenical Council: *When a Church Council is described as 'ecumenical' it is drawing on a Greek word meaning 'the whole inhabited world'*

Encyclical: *this simply means 'a circular letter'. An encyclical is a letter from the Pope to the Church, containing official teaching.*

Constitution, Dogmatic Constitution, Pastoral Constitution: *the four most important documents from the Second Vatican Council were called Constitutions, from the Latin 'constituere', 'to establish.' These teachings, of a pastoral or doctrinal nature are highly significant, 'establishing' the Church in this area.*

Final Prayer

Mary, Mother of the Redeemer, as we venture further into the Third Millennium, we ask that you will be for us the Star which safely guides our steps to the Lord. We ask this in the name of Jesus, your Son and Lord. Amen.

Session 4

Why the Catechism?

'Father... this is eternal life, that they may know You' (Jn 17:3)

Father, may the truth of the Gospel shine forth in your Church so that all are led by its beauty to seek you, the one God, and find everlasting life in your eternal Kingdom.
We ask this in the name of Jesus your Son, who lives and reigns with you and the Holy Spirit, world without end. Amen

In a previous session we discovered that a catechist is an echo of Christ and his Good News. We saw that the 'deposit of faith', as Scripture calls this treasure which is to be lovingly received and handed on, has been re-presented for our times in the Catechism of the Catholic Church. In this session we explore this Catechism. We look at its purpose, and how to use it for learning about the faith and for teaching the Faith.

The Catechism is a superbly-crafted teaching instrument. It is also a work that will transform your life and the lives of those you catechise. It is not a book to be read quickly; one needs to ponder the text, pray with it and immerse oneself in it to fully appreciate its visionary power and the compelling sense of beauty, goodness and truth which radiate from its pages. In these pages we meet the Spirit at work in his Church.

To read and use the Catechism prayerfully and carefully, searching its depths and allowing oneself to be questioned and challenged by its teaching, one needs to understand some of the elements which structure and inform its presentation of the faith. When these elements are firmly grasped and their significance appreciated the Catechism can become the most transforming and penetrating teaching tool the Church has ever possessed since the Scriptures.

Unfathomable riches

'I ask all the Church's Pastors and the Christian faithful to receive this Catechism in a spirit of communion and to use it assiduously in fulfilling their mission of proclaiming the faith and calling people to the Gospel life. This Catechism is given to them that it may be a sure and authentic reference text for teaching catholic doctrine... It is also offered to all the faithful who wish to deepen their knowledge of the unfathomable riches of salvation.'

Blessed Pope John Paul II, Fidei depositum, 'The Deposit of Faith'

The purpose of the Catechism

What do we learn about the Catechism from this excerpt from *Fidei depositum*?

1. • **It is a sure reference guide.** It is reliable, a secure point to which we can turn to discover and understand Church teaching. You can use the contents pages or the indices to find out about particular aspects of Church teaching.

   • **It proclaims faith.** It teaches the Faith clearly, unambiguously and fully. It is a serious presentation for adults of a living faith for today.

- **It calls us to the Gospel life, to Christ.** It is written to lead us to Christ and to life in him. The truths presented in its pages are truths about Christ. They lead us to communion with him.

- **It is a teaching tool.** The Catechism has been written to assist catechists, whether pastors or lay people. It is a teaching document. It is set out and structured for ease of teaching. It is the handbook every teacher of the Faith needs.

The logo on the front cover

2 Take a moment to look at the logo on the front cover of the Catechism. What is it? Look inside and read the explanation of the design. Notice how the logo presents the whole message of the Catholic Faith – Christ and His redemptive work are at the centre, redeemed humanity lies securely and peacefully at his feet, drawn into paradise to share the life of the Blessed Trinity. Christ is playing a beautiful melody, the 'symphony of the truth'.

This image of a **'symphony'** can help us to understand the **structure** and **layout** of the Catechism.

Structure

Just as a symphony normally has four movements, so the Catechism has four parts. These four parts correspond to the four 'parts', or dimensions, of the life of the Church and of every Christian. The Christian life is one of faith, worship, following Christ in the way we live, and prayer.

Catechism

3 **1. Turn to the Contents pages and *identify the four parts* of the Catechism.**

2. Notice the *ordering of the four parts* and the *amount of space* given to each. Parts 1 and 2 proclaim God's Revelation and work, his loving Plan of Salvation, through the time of the Old Testament, the New Testament and now in the time of the Church when he works through the Liturgy and the Sacraments. This is what we have faith in and what we celebrate. Parts 3 and 4 are concerned with our response to God's gracious activity – our life in Christ and our prayer. God's action comes first (parts 1 and 2) and two-thirds of the Catechism is concerned with presenting this for us. Our action follows as a response to what God has done, and just one-third explains what we are to do. The Catechism, then, emphasises God's grace in the Christian life and asks catechists to do the same.

3. Notice that each part of the Catechism has *two sections*. The first section in each case looks at general issues and points concerned with faith, worship, morality and prayer. The second section focuses upon the Creed, the Sacraments, the Commandments and the Our Father.

Layout and themes

A symphony is satisfying when it is experienced as a unified piece. A certain unity is achieved by the fact that the whole symphony is written in a particular musical key, C major, D minor, or whatever. Musical themes that are heard in one movement often recur in other movements.

We can think of the Catechism in a similar way. The authors of the Catechism tell us that 'This catechism is conceived as an *organic presentation* of the Catholic Faith in its entirety. It should therefore be seen as a unified whole.' (para 18) This is an important point. When we read a section of the Catechism we are doing more than learning about particular aspects of the Faith; the Catechism has been written so that, whichever page we open, we are introduced to the fullness of the Faith, to 'one thing' to be believed, to love and in which to place our hope. The Faith is one, though it is made up of many parts. This sense of unity is achieved in two ways in particular:

Through the use of cross-references. These link the different parts together to help us see connections between faith and life.

❹ What's on a page

This tells you which of the four parts of the Catechism you are in.

64

THE PROFESSION OF FAITH

history, governing hearts and events in keeping with his will: 'It is always in your power to show great strength, and who can withstand the strength of your arm?'[107]

'You are merciful to all, for you can do all things'[108]

2777   270   God is the *Father* Almighty, whose fatherhood and power shed light on one another: God reveals his fatherly omnipotence by the way he takes care of our needs; by the filial adoption that he gives us ('I will be a father to you, and you shall be my sons and daughters, says the Lord Almighty'):[109] finally by his infinite mercy, for he displays his power at its height by freely forgiving sins.

1441

271   God's almighty power is in no way arbitrary: 'In God, power, essence, will, intellect, wisdom, and justice are all identical. Nothing therefore can be in God's power which could not be in his just will or his wise intellect.'[110]

The mystery of God's apparent powerlessness

309
412
609
648

272   Faith in God the Father Almighty can be put to the test by the experience of evil and suffering. God can sometimes seem to be absent and incapable of stopping evil. But in the most *mysterious* way God the Father has revealed his almighty power in the voluntary humiliation and Resurrection of his Son, by which he conquered evil. Christ crucified is thus 'the power of God and the wisdom of God. For the foolishness of God is wiser than men, and the weakness of God is stronger than men.'[111] It is in Christ's Resurrection and exaltation that the Father has shown forth 'the immeasurable greatness of his power in us who believe'.[112]

148

273   Only faith can embrace the mysterious ways of God's almighty power. This faith glories in its weaknesses in order to draw to itself Christ's power.[113] The Virgin Mary is the supreme model of this faith, for she believed that 'nothing will be impossible with God', and was able to magnify the Lord: 'For he who is mighty has done great things for me, and holy is his name.'[114]

1814, 1817

274   'Nothing is more apt to confirm our faith and hope than holding it fixed in our minds that nothing is impossible with God. Once our reason has grasped the idea of God's almighty power, it

---

[107] *Wis* 11:21; cf. *Esth* 4:17b; *Prov* 21:1; *Tob* 13:2.
[108] *Wis* 11:23.
[109] 2 *Cor* 6:18; cf. *Mt* 6:32.
[110] St Thomas Aquinas, *STh* I, 25, 5, ad 1.
[111] 1 *Cor* 1:24-25.
[112] *Eph* 1:19-22.
[113] Cf. 2 *Cor* 12:9; *Phil* 4:13.
[114] *Lk* 1:37, 49.

Italicised words identify key teaching points, as do the bold sub-headings in the text.

When you are given a reference number for the Catechism, it is not the page number, but the paragraph number. All Church documents use this method of referencing. 'CCC' is the abbreviation used for the Catechism, so 'CCC 271' is paragraph number 271 in the Catechism.

The central truths of the Faith stand at the heart of every part of the Catechism: Christ, the Paschal Mystery, the Holy Trinity, the Church and the dignity of every human person.

The Catechism emphasises the implications for our lives of the Faith we profess, and provides models for us to contemplate.

These numbers point us to the sources which are listed at the foot of the page. Notice how the majority are from the Scriptures. Catechists can use these references for study, for memorisation and for prayer.

The numbers in italics at the side of the paragraphs are cross-references to other paragraphs. These shed more light on the topic you are considering. They expand points, link the parts together, and help to deepen our understanding of the topic we are investigating.

Look for these words - 'therefore', 'because', 'thus', 'for', and so on - which indicate that reasons are being given for the statement which has just been made. The Catechism explains the Faith as well as presenting it.

Through the use of recurring 'themes' which lie at the heart of the Faith. We can call these the 'foundational truths' of the Faith. They run like golden threads through each part of the Catechism. They are:

- The Holy Trinity
- The Person of Christ, true God and true Man
- The Paschal Mystery, the saving death and Resurrection of Christ
- The nature and dignity of the human person, created and graced

5 • The Church

One of the keys to effective teaching with the Catechism is to ensure that, whatever the subject you are teaching, you relate it to these key themes. Why? First, because in doing this you will be helping others to see the coherence of the faith, the way in which the pieces fit together. Secondly, because you will be offering your hearers reasons for the Faith: the Church's teaching becomes understandable in that the elements you are teaching are seen to be drawn together in a beautiful harmony around these themes.

6 Read paragraphs 214-221: 'God, He Who Is, is Truth and Love'.

Look for the points raised in this session.

Summary

In this third session we have been looking at:

- **Why the Catechism is so important for catechists**
- **How to use the Catechism to learn about the Faith**
- **How to use the Catechism to teach the Faith**

Further reading

- For the purpose of the Catechism: *'Fidei depositum'*, Blessed Pope John Paul II's introduction to the Catechism.
- For how to learn from the Catechism and teach the Faith from it: the Prologue, 1-25; and the General Directory for Catechesis, Part Two, Chapter Two.
- CCC 1996-1999: The Catechism on grace.

Glossary on some key terms in the new Catechism

Fidei depositum: *'Deposit of Faith', the title given by Blessed Pope John Paul II to his introduction to the Catechism*

Grace: *is a participation in the life of God, a free and undeserved gift. God's infinite love, always above and beyond us, but also revealed and therefore knowable by us to some extent*

Mystery: *the reality of God lying at the heart of creation and especially of the history of salvation which we know only because God has revealed himself to us*

Paschal Mystery: *the phrase used to describe the reality of our redemption through Christ's passion, Resurrection and Ascension, a redemption of which we know because God has revealed this to us.*

Final meditation and prayer

O my God, Trinity whom I adore, help me to forget myself entirely so as to establish myself in you, unmovable and peaceful as if my soul were already in eternity. May nothing be able to trouble my peace or make me leave you, O my unchanging God, but may each minute bring me more deeply into your mystery!
Blessed Elizabeth of the Trinity (see CCC 260)

Glory be to the Father, and to the Son and to the Holy Spirit. As it was in the beginning, is now, and ever shall be, world without end. Amen.

Session 5

Who Teaches?

**As the Father sent me so I send you
(John 20:21)**

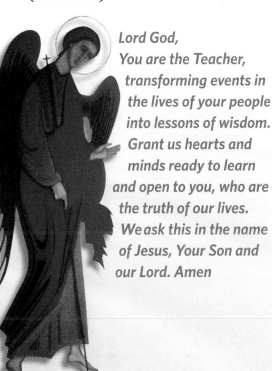

*Lord God,
You are the Teacher,
transforming events in
the lives of your people
into lessons of wisdom.
Grant us hearts and
minds ready to learn
and open to you, who are
the truth of our lives.
We ask this in the name
of Jesus, Your Son and
our Lord. Amen*

**The purpose of this session is to focus
on the supreme Catechist, God himself.
We rightly think of God as the subject
matter of our catechesis: our teaching
is about him. What we can easily forget,
though, is that the three Persons of the
Blessed Trinity are also actively present
in the mind and heart of the *catechist*,
in the work of *catechesis* and in the lives
of those being *catechised*. As catechists
we are deeply privileged in being able
to share in what is essentially a divine
work. This session will make clear how
much you can rely on God's presence and
providence in all catechetical activities.**

Let go and let God

'There is a temptation which perennially besets
every spiritual journey and pastoral work: that
of thinking that the results depend on our
ability to act and to plan. God, of course, asks
us really to co-operate with his grace...'
Blessed Pope John Paul II, NMI 38

God the Father: the Source of catechesis

God the Father is the Source of all that is. He is the
Source of the divine life of the Trinity. The infinite life
of the Trinity overflows, through sheer love and joy,
into the act of creation. The Father, then, is the Source
of everything that exists, and he wishes to give us, not
only a share in creation, but a share in his very own life.

From the first moment of our creation, therefore, God has
been working to draw us to himself. The principal way in
which he has done this has been by **revealing** himself and
his unchanging plan to draw us into his life of happiness.

God has revealed himself by sending his Son,
who shares in his own substance and being. The
source of our catechesis, then, lies in the Father's
desire to share his life with us. And this is why
all catechesis is rooted in Divine Revelation.

The Scriptures speak to us of God's desire that we should
come to know him and his love for us:

*'In many and various ways God spoke of old
to our fathers by the prophets; but in these last
days he has spoken to us by a Son, whom he
appointed the heir of all things.' (Hebrews 1:1)*

This text emphasises that **everything starts with
God's imaginative initiative** ('In many and various
ways') of entering into **dialogue** ('God spoke') for the
sake of a **relationship** with his people ('to us').

God teaches us in stages. First he teaches through the
prophets, and then he teaches fully through the Son,
the Word made flesh. Through the prophets God says,

*'Incline your ear, and come to me; hear
that your soul may live' (Is.55:3).*

And through the sending of his Son he calls out to us:

'This is my beloved Son, with whom I am well pleased: listen to him' (Matthew 17:5).

In catechesis, then, it is God who is constantly at work, making himself known.

Catechesis has its source in the Father's loving initiative to reveal himself and his plan by sending his Son.

Christ, sent by the Father

God **speaks** and **acts** in the person of Christ, who is the **Word** made **flesh**. In the person of Christ God has told us everything that he wants to say. Not only does Christ, like the prophets, speak words *from* God and *about* God, He *is* the Word of God. Not only does Christ, like the prophets before him and the saints after him, act as God wishes, He *is* God, acting in the flesh.

Christ is the bringer of the Good News, and he is the Good News itself. He teaches about God and his Kingdom, and he is himself the presence of God and his Kingdom among us. This is why he calls himself 'the Way and the Truth and the Life' (Jn 14:6).

① **Look at the following Scripture references from the Gospel of St. John showing Christ's union with the Father and his utter dependence upon him.**

- **5:19, 30**
- **6:57**
- **8:29**
- **12:49-50**
- **14:10, 24**

Pick out key words which indicate Christ's *union* with the Father and his *dependence* on him.

We have seen that the Father wants to establish a relationship with each person. He does this through sending God the Son. This is why the Church speaks of **communion** with Christ as the purpose of catechesis, because it is in and through communion with Christ that we are in communion with the Blessed Trinity. The Catechism opens with this verse from St John's Gospel: 'this is eternal life, that they know you, the only true God, and Jesus Christ whom you have sent.' (17:3)

Christ is at the centre of our teaching. The Church describes catechesis as 'Christocentric', 'Christ-centred'. In *Catechesi tradendae* we read:

- 'At the heart of catechesis we find, in essence, a person, the person of Jesus of Nazareth' (CT 5).
- 'In catechesis it is Christ... who is taught... everything else is taught in reference to him... and it is Christ alone who teaches... anyone else teaches to the extent that he is Christ's spokesman, enabling Christ to teach with his lips' (CT 6).

Christ is whom we teach. In a profound sense, Christ is also the Teacher, in fact the only true Teacher (cf. Mt 23:10). Catechesis has a divine source, accessible only through Christ who has come 'from above', as St John puts it (3:31). And so, as catechists, we are only teachers in so far as we live **in Christ**. Jesus said, 'Abide in me, and I in you... for apart from me you can do nothing' (Jn 15:4,5).

If we abide in Christ and live in communion with him in his Church we can teach with minds renewed in him (see Eph 4:23). Our teaching then flows from a relationship with Christ and knowledge of him. We teach effectively when the love of Christ controls our lives and the wisdom of Christ rules our minds. As we allow Christ to transform us, our lives and teaching match. The Word becomes flesh in us.

We can understand, then, the wisdom of Paul VI's words, 'The men of our day are more impressed by witnesses than by teachers, and if they listen to these it is because they also bear witness' *(Evangelii nuntiandi 41).*

❷ *To discuss together:* What are the means by which we can abide in Christ and continue to be transformed by Christ?

❸ *Listen* to the following adaptations from St John's Gospel. They will be read to you slowly and meditatively so that you can reflect on what it means to abide in Christ.

In catechesis it is Christ who is taught and Christ who teaches. The catechist abides in Christ.

The Holy Spirit

We have looked at the role of the Father as source of all revelation and Christ who was sent by the Father to reveal fully the mind, heart and plan of God. We have also seen that we are invited not simply to *learn from* him but also to *live in* him. In order to enable us to know Christ and to live in him, the Holy Spirit was sent to guide the Apostles.

In describing this mission that the Spirit would have in the Church, Christ used the significant words: 'The Holy Spirit whom the Father will send in my name will teach you everything and remind you of all I have said to you.' (Jn 14:26). And, he added: 'When the Spirit of Truth comes, he will lead you to the complete truth...' (Jn 16:13).

The Spirit is thus promised to the Church and to each Christian as an interior Teacher, who, through the light of faith, helps each person to grasp the reality of the truths of the Faith. The Holy Spirit is the Divine Teacher in every catechetical situation. Pope Paul VI therefore reminds us that we can never 'dispense with the secret action of the Holy Spirit' (EN 75).

Catechesi tradendae sums up these points when it says that, 'when carrying out her mission of giving catechesis, the Church – and also every individual Christian devoting himself to that mission within the Church and in her name – must be very much aware of acting as a living pliant instrument of the Holy Spirit. To invoke the Spirit constantly, to be in communion with Him... must be the attitude of the teaching Church and of every catechist' (CT 72).

The Holy Spirit is the interior Teacher of the Faith.

The Church

We have looked briefly at the role of the Persons of the Trinity in the work of catechesis. We must not forget the Church. The *General Directory for Catechesis* links the Church directly to the Holy Spirit in its heading: 'The transmission of Revelation by the Church, the work of the Holy Spirit' (GDC 42).

Catechesis is ecclesial (meaning 'of the Church') because the Holy Trinity continues its mission through the Church, of drawing humanity into the fullness of redemption. The *General Directory for Catechesis* says that, 'Continuing the mission of Christ and animated by the Holy Spirit, the Church is *the* teacher of the Faith. Catechesis is understood as an essentially ecclesial act' (GDC 78).

These are strong words and important for us to reflect upon. The Church transmits the Faith which she herself lives and, by this life and transmission, not only helps those being catechised, but also 'brings the community itself to maturity' (GDC 221).

Catechesis is also ecclesial because the Faith is always handed on in and through the Church. As individual Catholics, we have received the Faith of the Church and we now share in the passing on of this Faith.

Finally, catechesis is ecclesial because it is through the sacraments that we receive the grace we need to go out and spread the word. In this sacramental sense too, catechesis in the Faith of the Church is above all a work of grace and of the Church.

We join with the Holy Trinity and the Church in our work of catechesis.

Summary

In this fifth session we have been looking at:

- **The work of the Trinity in the catechist, in the work of catechesis, and in the lives of those being catechised.**

- **The desire and plan of the Father to draw us to himself through sending his Son among us.**

- **What it means to be 'in Christ', with Christ as the centre of catechesis.**

- **The work of the Holy Spirit in catechesis, in and through the Church.**

Further reading

On God the Father as the Source of catechesis:

- The opening paragraphs (1-4) of the Second Vatican Council document on Revelation, *Dei Verbum,* together with the Catechism 50-53, give us a clear presentation on why the Father wants to reveal himself to us and how he does this. The Scriptures emphasise the ways in which God continually intervenes to turn events into occasions of grace and wisdom. On this, read Jer 31:3 and Psalms 3, 18, 34, 81, 86, and 95.

On God the Son as the fullness of Truth:

- CCC 65, 428-9: give excellent summaries of this.

- GDC 40-41, 140: explain why catechesis must be Christocentric and examine the way in which Christ himself taught.

- CT 5-9: offers profound teaching on Christ the Catechist.

On God the Holy Spirit as the interior Teacher:

- CT 72 and GDC 142: examine the action of the Holy Spirit as the interior Teacher.

- CCC 683-686: explains the role of the Holy Spirit in awakening faith and ongoing conversion.

Glossary on the Trinity

Trinity: *One God in three persons, Father, Son and Holy Spirit, the central mystery of the Christian Faith.*

Revelation: *to make accessible or visible what was hidden. God reveals himself, makes himself known.*

Communion: *literally, 'union with.' The Divine Persons live in eternal communion, in union with each other.*

Christocentric: *Christ-centred.*

Christocentric catechesis: *catechesis centred on Christ.*

Ecclesial: *relating to the Church. The Church is the work of the Blessed Trinity, who fills her with grace.*

Abbreviations

From now on we will be using these abbreviations for the documents we have been considering:

CCC	*Catechism of the Catholic Church*
CT	*Catechesi tradendae*
DV	*Dei Verbum*
EN	*Evangelii nuntiandi*
GDC	*General Directory for Catechesis*

Final meditation and prayer

'Whoever is called to teach Christ must first seek "the surpassing worth of knowing Christ Jesus", he must suffer "the loss of all things..." in order to gain "Christ and be found in him..." ' (CCC 428)
God be in my head and in my understanding.
God be in my eyes and in my looking.
God be in my mouth and in my speaking.
God be in my heart and in my thinking.
God be at my end and at my departing. Amen.

Session 6

Whose Story?

'He interpreted for them all the scriptures' (Luke 24:27)

God our Father, We heard with our own ears, we have been told the story of the things you did long ago, the wonderful deeds which you performed. Send your Spirit upon your Church and do great deeds again in our time, O Lord, so that your power and wisdom, which you revealed in Christ, may be celebrated throughout the world. Amen.

In this session we look at the Catholic Story, the History of Salvation. This is the wonderful Story in which we find our true identity. As catechists we need to know this Story well and be able to communicate it to others. It is the context within which we place our teaching on all other matters.

Tell the Story

'The Church, in transmitting today the Christian message... has a constant memory of the saving events of the past and makes them known. In the light of these, she interprets the present events of human history, where the Spirit of God is continually renewing the face of the earth, and she waits with faith for the Lord's coming.'
GDC 107

From the beginning

From the earliest times in the Church we find that an essential part of catechesis has been telling others the Story of Creation and Salvation.

Let us look at one of the first instances. We find this in the Gospel of St Luke. After the crucifixion of Jesus the disciples were devastated. The One in whom they had placed all their hopes had been cruelly killed. To whom could they now turn in order to discover meaning and joy in their lives again? In Luke 24 we find two of the disciples walking out from Jerusalem to a small village called Emmaus. On their journey they are met by a stranger who walks alongside them.

Finding faith through the Story

1 **Listen to this passage, Luke 24:13-35.**

Notice how the two disciples are able to tell the last few days of the Story but do not have faith because they need to hear the whole of it. A small part, by itself, does not make sense to them. This whole Story is what Jesus tells them.

The Church calls this Story of Salvation the *'narratio'*, or 'narration'. It is the narrative of the Faith. What we believe is not primarily a set of timeless truths, but truths that we discover within a living history. The *General Directory for Catechesis* says that this Story, this history, read within the perspective of faith, is 'a fundamental part of the content of catechesis.' (GDC 108).

The Church's catechesis is placed within the story of salvation, the 'narratio'.

[Handwritten notes:]

ANNO DOMINI - YEAR OF THE LORD

[FINANCE - POWER - WAR (FORCE)]
SECULAR

GOD - CHURCH - SALVATION.

MOSES - LAW (FIRST 5 BOOKS OF OT)
PROPHETS

JESUS CHRIST (GENESIS CH 3
DEFEAT OF EVIL)
ISOLATING ISRAEL - TEACHING them humility

The point of the Story

This Story has love as its source, driving force, and goal.

'The whole concern of doctrine and its teaching must be directed to the love that never ends. Whether something is proposed for belief, for hope or for action, the love of our Lord must always be made accessible, so that anyone can see that all the works of perfect Christian virtue spring from love and have no other objective than to arrive at love' (CCC 25).

The role of the catechist, then, is to share with others the Story of God's never-ending love.

Coming to faith means coming to believe in the truth of this Story. And the Story is not outside of ourselves. It is *our* Story.

Every teaching we deliver, then, should flow from, and be directed towards, participation in the Catholic Story. For this Story includes, with the telling of it, an invitation to join the Catholic family and make the Story one's own.

The whole point of the Story, from beginning to end, is the love of God revealed in Christ.

The parts of the Story

The Story is grounded, of course, in the life of the Trinity:

'The whole history of salvation is identical with the history of the way and the means by which the one true God, Father, Son and Holy Spirit, reveals himself to men "and reconciles and unites with Himself those who turn away from sin" ' (CCC 234).

Like all good stories, the Catholic Story has a beginning, a middle and an end. The **beginning** is the act of Creation. The **middle** is the coming of Christ, his Incarnation, Life, death, Resurrection and Ascension. The **end** is the Second Coming of Christ, which ushers in the Final Judgement for the whole of humanity.

These give us the key marker points in the Story. They tell us where we must start and finish and where the Story reaches its central climax – in the redemptive life and work of Christ.

The *General Directory for Catechesis* describes the main sections of the Story, through which God has revealed himself to us, as:

'the great stages of the **Old Testament** by which God prepared the journey of the Gospel; **the life of Jesus**, Son of God, born of the Virgin Mary, who by his actions and teaching brought Revelation to completion; **the history of the Church** which transmits Revelation.' (108)

The three stages of the Story are the times of the Old Testament starting with Creation, the New Testament, and the history of the Church ending with the Second Coming.

Telling the Story

What are the main points that make up the Story? Let us look at the sections of the Story in more detail now. We can examine this unfolding of Revelation, as God reaches for us throughout Salvation History, within the overall three stages.

2 **The first stage: Creation, the Fall and the Promise of Salvation**

- God our uncreated Creator, is a Trinity, a family of Persons, who has a plan for us
- God created all things, visible and invisible. We emphasise the goodness of creation, humanity being created in God's image, and the creation of angels
- The Fall: sin, death, and the corruption of the human family's relationship with God. We also speak of the loss of harmony between people and between humanity and creation
- God's gathering of a people to himself: the covenants with Noah, Abraham, Moses and David as steps towards the restoration of communion
- God's promises through the Prophets of the establishing of a new relationship, a new covenant

The second stage: the Life of God the Son

- The Incarnation: Jesus is true God and true Man. This is the centre of the Story
- Mary's unique participation in God's gift of himself, her 'yes' to God, the supreme example of grace working to bring about human cooperation with God's plan
- Jesus' preaching and teaching on the Kingdom of God in which all things will be restored
- The Paschal Mystery: Jesus' Suffering, Death, Resurrection and Ascension for our redemption

- The establishing of the universal Church in which God re-gathers us again in Christ

The third stage: the Era of the Church

- The Descent of the Holy Spirit at Pentecost: he is the guarantor of the deposit of faith and the life of the deposit of grace
- The Story since Pentecost: a new family identity, the saints, all of us here and now
- Our 'waiting in joyful hope' for the coming of Christ. We live in expectation. The Church calls this part of the Story the time of the *'expectatio'*, the awaiting
- The Second Coming of Jesus and Heaven

Identifying the parts

3 **Look at the Creed which we say at Mass and identify the three stages of the narratio, of the Catholic Story.**

Now look carefully at the extract from Eucharistic Prayer 4 and find the *narratio* there.

It is important to know clearly the outline of the Story of Salvation, from beginning to end.

The Story in the Catechism

The *General Directory for Catechesis* speaks of seven 'foundation stones' or 'basic elements' which need to lie at the heart of all catechesis. We find all of them in the Catechism.

Four of these foundation stones are the four parts of the Catechism. As you know, these four parts correspond to the four dimensions of the Christian life:

- the Profession of Faith (Part 1)
- the Celebration of the Mystery (Part 2)
- Life in Christ (Part 3)
- Christian Prayer (Part 4)

These are the four pillars of the Christian life: we believe, worship, live and pray.

The other three foundation stones are 'the three phases in the narration of the history of salvation' (GDC 130): the Old Testament, the life of Jesus and the history of the Church.

The General Directory for Catechesis asks us to set our expositions of the Faith, worship life and prayer of the Church *within* this narrative framework. In other words, when we catechise and explain the truths of Catholic faith and life we are helping our hearers to understand these things as elements within a story, a story in which they share.

The Catechism and the Story

4 **Look at the way in which the Catechism places its teaching on Baptism within the framework of the History of Salvation CCC 1217-1226. Other examples of how the Catechism places doctrine within the Story of Salvation are listed in the further reading.**

The Catechism models for us the setting of our teaching within the narratio.

Using the Story in catechesis

Finally, let us look at some practical ideas about using the Story in our handing on of the Faith.

- Telling the Story could take just five minutes, it could take thirty minutes or it could be examined more in-depth and take as long as time allows. The way in which we tell the Story, what we select, what we omit and what we choose to emphasise, depends to a large extent on the particular situation and audience. We need to practice telling the Story in a variety of situations.

- All those whom we catechise need to know this Story and be invited to make it their own. Tell the Story using 'our', 'we' and 'us' to make it clear that it really is the Story of the Catholic 'family'.

- It is often helpful to use beautiful and striking art to illustrate and bring home the Story. Pictures can be powerful and people often remember points better once they are linked to visual images.

- The Catholic Story needs to inform all that we hand on. Repeating the Story to a group in a number of different ways can often be beneficial, reinforcing ideas for the group. Tell the Story early in your catechesis so that everything that is heard subsequently can be placed within this framework. Then tell the Story again towards the end – those you are catechising will listen to the Story with new knowledge and understanding.

- Remember the overall purpose of telling the Story – to open us to the love and grace of God so that we can share in his life and love, see what is involved in becoming perfect in love as the 'heavenly Father is perfect' (Matt 5:48) and come to the glory of the Trinity. By keeping the purpose of the Story in mind, each truth we learn becomes an episode in the continuing Story of God's love for us.

We learn the Story well so that we can tell it in a number of different ways.

Summary

In this fifth session we have been looking at:

- **The Catholic Story, the History of Salvation.**
- **The main parts of this Story and the key teaching points we need to emphasise.**
- **The Story as it is presented in the Scriptures and the Catechism.**

- **Why we need to know this Story well and place our teaching within this History of Salvation**
- **The fact that we need to invite those we are catechising to make this Story the one in which they, too, find their identity**
- **The love of the Holy Trinity as the source and goal of all things**

Further reading

- CCC 54-67 sets out the basic salvation history. The Scriptural verses referred to here are helpful for developing the outline of the story.
- Psalms 105 and 136 are examples of early recountings of the story in the Old Testament.
- The Benedictus (Luke 1:67-79) and the speech of the first martyr, Stephen (Acts 7:2-53) are examples of New Testament tellings of the story.
- Other examples from the Catechism where doctrine is placed within the Story of Salvation are: The Church (CCC 758-769), The Holy Spirit (CCC 702-741) and The Eucharist (CCC 1333-1344).

Glossary on the Story

Covenant: *spousal promise of faithfulness.*

Narratio: *the narrative, or Story, of our salvation*

Expectatio: *the period in which we now live as we await the second coming of Christ.*

Catholic: *universal, whole; the Catholic Story is the whole story for all to join, from Adam to the last human being.*

Final meditation and prayer

Mary, you stand at the heart of God's plan for our salvation. Because of your 'yes' to God, the Word was made flesh and came to dwell among us. You live now in the glory of the Holy Trinity. Pray for us, that we may come to share in that same glory and know the fulfilment of God's plan for our lives. We ask this in the name of your Son, Jesus Christ, our Lord. Amen.

Session 7

Who are we?

'You shall be consecrated to me'
Exodus 22:31

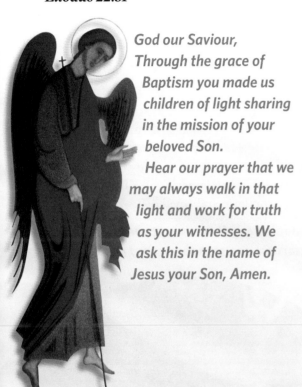

God our Saviour,
Through the grace of
Baptism you made us
children of light sharing
in the mission of your
beloved Son.
Hear our prayer that we
may always walk in that
light and work for truth
as your witnesses. We
ask this in the name of
Jesus your Son, Amen.

In the last session, we were looking at our Story, the Story which we join by Baptism into Christ, and it is in virtue of our rebirth in Christ that we also share Christ's mission. Christ's mission is described from the earliest times as that of Priest, Prophet and King. In this session we answer the question, 'who are we?' by exploring what it means for us, in the Church, to be Priest, Prophet and King in Christ.

In the Church this mission is shared by the clergy and the lay faithful in different but complementary ways, 'for in the Church there is diversity of ministry but unity of mission' (CCC 873). We will therefore need to look at who we are in relation to the ordained ministers especially the parish priest and permanent deacons.

'Jesus Christ is the one whom the Father anointed with the Holy Spirit and established as priest, prophet and king. The whole People of God participates in these three offices of Christ and bears the responsibilities for mission and service that flow from them.' (CCC 783)

Priest, Prophet and King

The word 'Christ' comes from the Hebrew word meaning 'anointed'. In the Old Testament we find three types of people who were anointed which meant that they were consecrated or set apart to help in God's mission. The three types of people were prophets, priests and kings and so Christ, as the perfect one fulfilling God's mission completely, is understood by the Church as *perfect* Priest, *perfect* Prophet and *perfect* King.

Christ's mission, then, from the earliest times, has been understood as a unity of these three roles. These three roles sum up his mission. They are also united in his body, the Church, and sum up the Church's mission.

- The priest makes sacrifices and offers worship to God – in the Church this is called the sanctifying office.
- The prophet is one who proclaims or teaches the Word of God – in the Church this is called the teaching office.
- The king directs the lives of the people in accordance with God's laws – in the Church this is called the governing office.

We will consider what sharing in Christ's priestly, prophetic and royal office means for us in practice. Firstly, however, we will look at these offices in the light of the diversity of ministry that exists in the Church.

The roles of priest, prophet and king sum up Christ's and the Church's mission.

Common Priesthood of the faithful and the Ministerial Priesthood

There is a very important sentence from the Council document *Lumen gentium,* for understanding the [VATICAN II COUNCIL] difference between those who are ordained (permanent deacons, priests, bishops) and those who are lay people (parents, catechists etc.). The common priesthood of the faithful and the ministerial priesthood (ordained) 'though they differ essentially and not only in degree... are none the less ordered one to another; [since] each in its own proper way shares in the one priesthood of Christ' (LG 10).

The **ministerial priesthood** is at the service of the **common priesthood** that we all share. The ministerial priesthood 'ministers', that is, it serves, supports, leads, governs, teaches, builds and nourishes the common priesthood of all the faithful. Without the ministerial priesthood, without that 'sacred ministering', the common priesthood cannot function properly. Without lay participation, the ministerial priesthood does not function properly either.

'The ministerial priesthood is a means by which Christ unceasingly builds up and leads his Church. For this reason it is transmitted by its own sacrament, the Sacrament of Holy Orders' (CCC 1547).

The common priesthood and ministerial priesthood share in different ways in the one priesthood of Christ.

The mission of the laity

The Fathers of The Second Vatican Council developed a vision of the laity as those who can permeate the secular world with the Spirit of Christ. This is possible through bearing witness in their personal, family and social lives by proclaiming and sharing the gospel of Christ in the situations in which they find themselves, and by their involvement with the task of explaining, defending, and applying Christian principles to the problems of today's world.

In addition to this, the lay faithful may be called to *assist* in the sacred ministry of the clergy (especially as readers, catechists and extraordinary ministers of Holy Communion). Since these tasks are most closely linked to the duties of pastors, that is, ordained ministers, it is necessary to remember:

- that the ordained minister (usually a priest, sometimes a deacon) remains ultimately responsible in these areas
- that 'collaboration with' the priest does not mean 'substitution for' him
- that care should be taken to safeguard the nature and mission of sacred ministry
- that care should be taken to safeguard the vocation and proper character of the lay faithful
- that the training received by the priest over many years is an indication of the seriousness of the ministry in the eyes of the Church reminding lay people that training is absolutely essential for them too
- that lay participation here is to a limited degree and in a prescribed manner.

Because many dioceses are looking to the laity to provide increased assistance in parishes, it may be helpful to look at the role of the parish and the parish priest before we consider lay participation in Christ's priestly, prophetic and royal office.

Lay people have their own proper calling and can also assist in the sacred ministry.

The Parish and the Parish Priest

In general, the parish is the local manifestation of the universal Church. The Code of Canon Law defines the parish as: 'A certain community of Christ's faithful ... whose pastoral care, under the authority of the diocesan bishop, is entrusted to its parish priest as its proper pastor' (canon 515).

The parish priest is the proper pastor of the parish entrusted to him, under the diocesan bishop, so that for his community he may carry out the offices of sanctifying, teaching and ruling with the co-operation of other priests and deacons and with the assistance of lay members in accordance with the law (see canon 519).

1 Fill in the chart below with what you think they should be be. In the first two columns write in the ministry and office. In the next 4 columns write in the type of participation using one of the 4 symbols. 3 are filled in to help you get started.

CHRIST'S THREEFOLD MINISTRY OF PROPHET, PRIEST AND KING
As exercised in the three offices of the Church – Teaching, Sanctifying and Governing

Action	Office of the Church	Ministry of Christ	Bishop	Priest	Deacon	Lay Person
To own church property	Governing	King	✓			
To make legal decisions	Governing	King	✓	✓		
To decide parish policy	Governing	King	■	■		
To preside at Mass	Sanctifying	Priest	✓	✓	⦸	
To proclaim the Gospel at Mass	Teaching	Prophet	■	■	■	
To proclaim a homily at Mass	Teaching	Prophet	✓	✓	✓	
To preach at any other time or occasion	Teaching	Prophet	✓	✓	✓	✓
To read the First and Second Readings	Teaching	Prophet	✓	✓	✓	✓
To read the Bidding Prayers	Sanctifying	Priest		✓		✓
To distribute Holy Communion	Sanctifying	Priest	✓	✓	✓	✓
To prepare someone for Baptism	Teaching	Prophet	✓	✓	✓	✓
To preside at the Sacrament of Baptism	All Three	All Three	■	■	■	●
To preside at the Sacrament of Confirmation	All Three	All Three	✓	✓		
To prepare someone for the Sacrament of Marriage	Teaching	Prophet	✓	✓	✓	✓
To preside at Sacrament of Holy Orders	Sanctifying	King		✓	✓	
To preside at the Sacrament of the Sick	Sanctifying	Priest				
To give Communion to the sick and housebound	Sanctifying	Prophet		✓	✓	✓
To prepare for the Sacrament of Reconciliation	Teaching	Prophet			✓	✓
To preside at the Sacramant of Reconciliation	All Three	Priest		✓		
To administer a funeral service, burial or cremation	Sanctifying	Priest	✓	✓		
To prepare someone for the Sacrament of the Eucharist	Teaching	Prophet		✓		
To expose the Blessed Sacrament with Benediction	Sanctifying	Priest		✓	✓	
To expose the Blessed Sacrament with simple Exposition				✓	✓	
To lead the Stations of the Cross	Teaching	Prophet		✓	✓	✓
To lead Morning and Evening Prayer	All 3			✓	✓	
To participate in the offertory procession	Sanctifying	Priest				✓
To lead or help with the Children's Liturgy	Teaching	Prophet		✓	✓	✓
To serve at the altar	Sanctifying	Priest			✓	✓
To prepare the parish newsletter	Teaching	Priest		✓		✓
To clean or help maintain the church building and grounds	Governing					✓
To arrange flowers in the church	Governing					✓
To lead or help with RCIA	Teaching	Priest		✓	✓	

■ participates in the ministry of Christ expressed in the offices of the Church
▶ participates usually as part of a parish team and with training
● may participate in extraordinary circumstances and with training
▲ may participate in this way but it would be unusual

Canon Law also establishes a parish as a juridical person (canon 515). In other words the 'parish' is the person responsible in law, which means that the people in the parish are not subject to legal rights and obligations, the 'parish' is. It is the parish priest who represents the parish.

The collaboration of the faithful with the priest in his pastoral ministry should lead to an enrichment of the Church but it is necessary to have a clear understanding of both the non-ordained and ordained person's participation in Christ's mission in order to achieve a harmonious, working relationship which results in the building up of the Church.

Clarity about roles and responsibilities is vital for fruitful catechesis in the parish.

Summary:

In this session we have looked at:

- **The participation of the laity in the three offices of Christ: Priest, Prophet and King.**

- **An explanation of the common priesthood of the faithful and the ministerial priesthood.**

- **The nature of the parish and the role of the Parish Priest.**

- **How the laity can assist the priest in his Sacred Ministry.**

Further Reading

- GDC 230-232: the roles of the lay catechist explained.

- CCC 888-896: covers the teaching, sanctifying and governing offices in the Church.

- CCC 897-900: the Church's teaching on the laity.

- CCC 901 to 913: what it means for the laity to participate in Christ's mission.

Glossary of words associated with Parish Mission

Mission: *from the Latin word 'missio' meaning 'I send'. 'Mission' is what Christ and the Church are sent by God the Father to do, in the power of the Holy Spirit. We share the one mission of the Trinity.*

Ministry: *from the Latin word 'munus' meaning 'service'. 'Sacred Ministry' is the title given to the service of ordained ministers because of the sacred power by which they act.*

Office: *a function or position in the Church founded in either divine or Church law and exercised for a spiritual purpose.*

Pastor, Pastoral: *'pastor' comes from the Latin word for shepherd. A shepherd guards over and leads the flock, and so pastoral ministry is similar to the kingly office of Christ. Christ lives his kingship as a good shepherd.*

Juridical person: *the one responsible before the law. The one responsible does not have to be an individual human person but can be a group (like school governors), or a group that is represented by someone, as a parish is by the parish priest.*

Code of Canon Law: *The Code of Canon Law is a book of regulations drawn from the life of the Church and is written to make clear the roles and responsibilities necessary in the Spirit-filled life of the Church.*

Closing Prayer

Holy Spirit, fill our hearts that they may grow in your gifts enabling us to develop our full potential in this life. May we be filled with your abundance and love, finding fulfilment and happiness whilst seeking always the values of the Gospel and the well being of others. Amen.

Session 8

Why link with the liturgy?

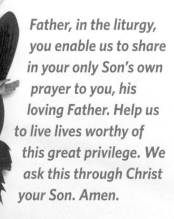

Christ, our spiritual and eternal sacrifice
(Cf. Heb 9:14)

Father, in the liturgy, you enable us to share in your only Son's own prayer to you, his loving Father. Help us to live lives worthy of this great privilege. We ask this through Christ your Son. Amen.

In this session we look first of all at why we should link catechesis with the liturgy. We also consider what liturgy is and examine some of the key elements of liturgy which are important for our catechesis. Finally, we look at three practical ways of making our catechesis liturgical.

The reasons

For the Catholic Church 'every liturgical celebration, because it is an action of Christ the priest and of his body, which is the Church, is a sacred action surpassing all others' (SC7).

We need to consider this striking statement from the Second Vatican Council's teaching on the liturgy, *Sacrosanctum concilium* (SC), very carefully. We can see from the statement that liturgy is not just the Catholic way of organising a weekly religious service of prayer. Liturgy is called a 'sacred action' and one which 'surpasses' all others. You will already have an idea of what liturgy is, so, before we look at this in more detail, let us consider a brief initial answer to the question being asked in this session.

In our catechesis we link to liturgy for three main reasons:

- Firstly, catechesis needs to be **about the liturgy**, since it is important for everyone to know what is happening in liturgical celebrations, sacred actions surpassing all others.

So, we need to be able to say what the priest and people do and why they do it, what the symbols and actions in liturgy are and what they signify.

- Secondly, all catechesis is to **lead people to participation in the liturgy** because the liturgy is the summit towards which all the activity of the Church is directed and the fount from which all her power flows (SC10).

So, we need to be able to say when the feasts and great celebrations of the liturgical year are and help others to be prepared for them.

- Thirdly, **the liturgy itself is catechesis** in its most profound form. The liturgy teaches by experience and gives what it teaches. It not only presents the mystery of Christ sacramentally, it also lets us immediately partake of his mystery.

So, we need to invite people to liturgy in the parish. We can know that bringing people into the liturgy is equivalent to bringing them into the presence of Christ.

We will look at the main points of each of these links with the liturgy but firstly let us look in more detail about what liturgy is.

It is essential that our catechesis be liturgical.

What is liturgy?

Liturgy is the public participation of the people of God in the work of God (see CCC 1069).

Many have a very limited view of liturgy as simply rules and regulations (the rubrics) which are connected to each of the celebrations of the Church's sacraments. But the Church's own understanding of liturgy, as we have seen, is that it is 'an action surpassing all others'. Liturgy is actually about the Trinity's work of Redemption and how this is communicated to the world today.

The liturgy is the worship which the Church renders to the Father through Jesus our High Priest, in the unity of the Holy Spirit. It is the worship offered by the mystical body of Christ, head and members – that is, Christ and his people.

Liturgy, then, is the communal prayer of the 'whole Christ'. Liturgy includes:

- the Eucharist, the highest form of liturgy

- the liturgy of the other sacraments

- the 'Liturgy of the Hours', or the 'Divine Office'. This is the name given to the official daily Prayer of the Church. It is largely composed of the Psalms, together with other scriptural and spiritual readings

- the Liturgy of Benediction.

We need to remember, then, that liturgy is first and foremost God's work, in and with and through his people gathered together. God comes among his people to bless them and to share his grace. Liturgy is at the heart of all Catholic life, the life of a people united with God in worship and praise.

Liturgy is our participation in the redemptive work of God.

In more detail

Let us look at five aspects of liturgy that are always important.

1. The Liturgical Year
The liturgy of the Eucharist and the Divine Office are organised each year principally around the life of Christ, from conception and birth, Baptism, temptation and Transfiguration, to Death, Resurrection and Ascension. This is called 'the Liturgical Year'. Within this cycle we also celebrate Our Lady, the apostles and the saints – some of the members of Christ's family, of *our* family in Christ.

The Liturgical year starts on the first Sunday of Advent. During the course of the year, Catholics follow, day by day, week by week, and by means of liturgical seasons and festivals, the story of salvation history, 'the Story' which we looked at in a previous session. The readings, hymns and prayers are arranged so that the story of Christ's work of redemption is unfolded like the chapters of a book.

At the heart of the Liturgical year is the Lord's resurrection. This stands at the centre of the faith, and therefore of the liturgy also. For this reason, Easter is the crown of the Liturgical year. All the other celebrations of the Church's year draw their meaning from Easter. The Church thinks of every Sunday as a 'mini' Easter Sunday.

The seasons of the Liturgical Year support us in our journey into God and the transformation of our lives. By steeping us in the mysteries of Christ they change 'time' into 'sacred time'.

What is past in time is *present* in sacred time, which is God's time. In the liturgy, what is past is made present. The Church teaches us that every day is the 'today' of God. This belief is reflected in the prayers of the liturgy. So, for example, a prayer for the day of Pentecost says, '*This* is the day of Pentecost, alleluia. *Today* the Holy Spirit appeared to the disciples in the form of fire and gave them his special gifts ..' (Magnificat antiphon, Evening Prayer II, Pentecost; *italics added*).

1 **Can you think of examples of how to link catechetical sessions to the Liturgical Year?**

Arranging catechesis around the Liturgical Year is a way of sharing in the life of Christ in his Church and coming closer to him.

2. Prayer and liturgy
In the liturgy we are privileged to join with Christ in his act of love and self-offering to the Father. Liturgical prayers are the prayers of Christ the head united to his body, the Church. They are:

- prayers in the liturgy to God the Father led by the priest, who represents Christ, the Son of God

- prayers spoken or sung by the priest and people together, or in dialogue.

2 Can you think of examples of liturgical prayers that everyone would benefit from knowing by heart?

Include liturgical prayers in catechesis. Explain them, learn them by heart and pray them together.

3. Liturgical signs and symbols

The liturgy is more than prayers. Just as human languages include physical signs and gestures, so the Church's liturgical language includes signs such as the bread and wine which will become the Body and Blood of Christ, symbolic materials such as water and oil, and gestures such as genuflecting, processing, and the Sign of the Cross. These signs, actions and symbols are powerful non-verbal forms of catechesis.

3 Can you think of other examples of signs, gestures and symbols that could be explained?

In catechesis we can explain the meanings of the signs and symbols so that they can be experienced more fully.

4. Liturgical readings

Liturgical readings are always taken from the Scriptures in the Mass and other

Sacraments, and from Scripture and Tradition in the Divine Office. The Church has brought together a wide selection of carefully-chosen readings from the whole Bible for the yearly cycle: the book of this collection is called the Lectionary (from the Latin word *'lectio'* which means 'I read'). Mass readings are always to be taken from here.

Catechesis that uses the liturgical readings helps to insert people into the liturgy where we listen to the Word of God.

5. Liturgical colours

Colour coding is used frequently in the secular world to help instant recognition in various circumstances. Think, for example, of the use of blue for 'cold' and red for 'stop, danger, hot'. The Church has her own method of colour coding according to the liturgical season and feast day, to help us to identify with the Mysteries of Christ in his Church.

4 *It is good to know and use the liturgical colours as part of one's way of catechising.*

Liturgical catechesis

The Church 'ardently desires that all the Christian faithful be brought to that full, conscious and active participation which is required by the very nature of the liturgy and the dignity of the baptismal priesthood' (GDC 85).

Now that we have looked at what liturgy is and some of its elements, we can examine more fully what our catechesis might include for it to be liturgical.

Linked to liturgy in its content

We can teach carefully and fully about the liturgy.

'Liturgical catechesis aims to initiate people into the mystery of Christ by proceeding from the visible to the invisible, from the sign to the thing signified, from the Sacraments to the mysteries' (CCC 1075).

Linked to liturgy in its spirit

Our catechesis can be informed with a 'liturgical spirit', so that we are continually leading people to the liturgy of the Church where they will be able to receive Christ.

For this reason catechesis, as well as developing knowledge and understanding of the liturgy and the sacraments, must also educate the disciples of Jesus Christ in an attitude of loving respect

- for prayer - private and public
- for thanksgiving
- for repentance
- for confidence in prayer
- for community spirit

since all of this 'is necessary for a true liturgical life' (see GDC 85).

Linked to liturgy in its planning

Planning has to do with the use of time. God created time for the same reason that he created everything else: so that he could use it to lead us to salvation. We can plan our catechesis carefully so that our topics link to the Liturgical year and encourage participation in the Church's liturgy.

In this way our catechesis is linked to sacred time.

To help you, it is a good idea to use a Catholic diary. This will have all the dates of the Church's Liturgical Year, its seasons and feast days. (The Diocesan Directory or Diocesan *Ordo* will also have the special feast days and the liturgical colours for your particular diocese). By noting these as you plan catechetical sessions you are already beginning to see time in a sacred way, to see time as the Church sees it, and to link sessions to seasons and liturgical celebrations. Such planning builds the parish as a worshipping community.

Summary

In this eighth session we have been considering:

- **why catechesis needs to be liturgical.**
- **what liturgy is and what are some of its important elements for catechesis.**
- **three practical ways of making catechesis more liturgical.**

Further Reading

- CCC 1066-1075: the Catechism explains the basics about the liturgy and the importance of liturgical catechesis.
- CCC 1163-1173: the liturgical year explained.

Glossary on the Liturgy

Sacrosanctum concilium **(SC):** *the document from the Second Vatican Council on the Liturgy.*

Redemption: *the work of the Holy Trinity saving us through the Life, Death and Resurrection of Christ. This work of Redemption is made present to us, and 'applied' to us, in the sacrifice of the Mass.*

Benediction: *A time of adoration of the Blessed Sacrament outside of the Mass which concludes with the blessing (benediction) of those present.*

Lectionary: *the Cycle of Readings chosen to accompany the Mass. The Sunday readings are organized around a three-year cycle: Year A (St Matthew), Year B (St Mark) and Year C (St Luke). Parts of St John are read during each year. The weekday readings are organized around a two-year cycle.*

Sacred time: *God's time, into which we enter in the liturgy. What is past in time is made present in God's time.*

Signs and symbols: *physical realities through which we communicate with other people and with God.*

Final Prayer

Almighty and everliving God,
by whose Spirit the whole body of the Church is governed and sanctified:
hear our prayer which we offer for all your faithful people, that each in his vocation and ministry may serve you in holiness and truth to the glory of your Name.
We ask this through Christ our Lord.
Amen.

Session 9

What is the Mystery?

'Worship the Father in Spirit and in Truth' (Jn 4:23)

Come, Lord Jesus! Come in the sacraments and liturgy, come in our lives, and come in Your heavenly glory! Amen.

In this session our topic is the Mystery, the mystery of the life of God himself, the life of the Blessed Trinity. It includes God's plan of unfathomable love for us, a plan for our good, our salvation through Christ. In its fullest sacramental form the mystery is made present for us in the Mass. Here, we look at how this Mystery of love is the source and purpose of the liturgy and also the source and purpose of our catechesis. All catechesis is given in order to insert us more fully into the Mystery.

The Mystery

The Church uses the word 'mystery' in a very particular way in liturgy. 'Mystery' is always:

- **divine** and therefore it is always above and beyond us. But it is also

- **revealed** and therefore it is knowable by us to some extent. What we know from revelation is true but always known in a limited way. We can know truly about God's mystery but never know fully.

- **merciful** love. God always reveals his divine mystery as merciful and loving.

God's mystery is revealed as the merciful plan of the Trinity, a plan of unfathomable love.

'By natural reason man can know God with certainty, on the basis of his works. But there is another order of knowledge, which man cannot possibly arrive at by his own powers: the order of divine Revelation. Through an utterly free decision, God has revealed himself and given himself to man. This he does by revealing the mystery, his plan of loving goodness, formed from all eternity in Christ, for the benefit of all men. God has fully revealed this plan by sending us his beloved Son, our Lord Jesus Christ, and the Holy Spirit.' (CCC 50)

❶ From your reading of this quotation:

what is the mystery?

why did God reveal it?

how did God reveal it?

So, when we read or hear phrases with another word attached to 'mystery', such as 'Paschal Mystery', we must remember that this is the divine, merciful love of God that is revealed in something to us so that we can get a glimpse of something far beyond us. (In the case of the Paschal Mystery it is revealed in Jesus' Passion, death, Resurrection and Ascension.)

Mystery is God's infinite love revealed and made visible.

Catechesis and the mystery

In catechesis we speak about the mystery of God, of all that God has revealed to us in Christ. As we do so we remember that the full reality of Christ and of God always lies far beyond what we can understand or communicate. And so we catechise with a profound sense of awe and reverence before the mystery we proclaim.

We saw in the last session that the liturgy actually gives, makes present, the mystery about which we teach. The Catechism speaks of the time since Pentecost as that of the 'dispensation of the mystery' – in other words, the time during which 'Christ manifests, makes present and communicates his work of salvation through the liturgy of his Church' (CCC 1076). During this time the Lord acts through the sacraments: they make present for us the Redemption which he has won. Because of this, the Catechism describes the sacraments and liturgy as the 'privileged place' for catechising the People of God.

Our catechesis should lead people into the presence of the mystery.

The centre of the mystery

The centre of the mystery is God's infinite love made present for us. This revelation and making present takes place in a manner surpassing all others in the Eucharist. The Second Vatican Council calls the Eucharist 'the source and summit of the Christian life' (LG 11) and the Catechism describes the Eucharist as 'the sum and summary of our faith' (CCC 1327).

We will therefore examine aspects of the Eucharist and its celebration. Reflecting upon these will guide us in our catechesis so that it truly leads others to a deeper participation in the Mystery.

By 'participation' the Church does not mean 'as much outward activity as possible', but, rather, an inward involvement, by attentiveness to, and faith in, what is happening in the liturgy.

Our catechesis is to be orientated towards a deep participation in the Eucharist.

Worship: our response to the Sacred Mystery

We saw in the last session that the Holy Trinity is at work in the liturgy. In the liturgy the mystery of God is revealed to our minds and our senses. We see the Father, the Son and the Holy Spirit at work for our redemption. The centre of this work is the Eucharist.

In the Eucharist we share in the worship which the Church renders to the Father through Jesus our High Priest, by the power of the Holy Spirit.

Faced with the mystery, our response is worship. This is the approach we take to God who reveals himself. What he reveals evokes praise, thanksgiving, reverence and awe.

Worship is our response to the mystery.

The church building for the sacred mystery

We must remember that the interior of a church is not just a container to be filled as we like. The Catechism defines a church as:

'a house of prayer in which the Eucharist is celebrated and reserved, where the faithful assemble, and where is worshipped the presence of the Son of God our Saviour, offered for us on the sacrificial altar for the help and consolation of the faithful – this house ought to be in good taste and a worthy place for prayer and sacred ceremonial. In this 'house of God' the truth and the harmony of the signs that make it up should show Christ to be present and active in this place.' (CCC 1181)

The church is built up from its centre, its heart, which is the altar. The altar is the place where the sacrifice of the Cross is made present. Closely connected to this is the tabernacle where Christ may be continually adored. Nearby is the lectern from which Christ's Word is proclaimed. Christ in his paschal mystery, then, is the central point in every church, and it is around him that the congregation assembles, building up the Body of Christ and centring all our worship of God around the altar.

Explaining these points helps to provide an answer to those who ask why we need to go to a church to worship.

❷ Can you think of actions which indicate the sacredness of the altar?

Awareness of the mystery will enable us to recover a 'sense of the sacred' in all that surrounds our worship. He is with us!

Sharing in the mystery of heaven

Christian worship is earthly, using the things of this world and all natural, human talents. At the same time it is heavenly because it brings us into the presence of God. When we on earth celebrate the liturgy, especially the liturgy of the Mass. We sing the Holy, Holy, Holy Lord with the whole Church in heaven. We offer the Eucharistic sacrifice with Mary, the Mother of God and with all the saints. In our small parish church we are united to heaven.

3 How aware are we that the earthly liturgy we celebrate in our parishes is participation in the liturgy of heaven?

The Eucharist is celebrated by the 'whole Christ', head and body, that is with all the saints and angels in the heavenly kingdom.

Misunderstandings of the mystery of the Eucharist

In our catechesis it is helpful to anticipate, and respond to, misunderstandings about the topic we are teaching. In the case of the Mass these misunderstanding often include the following areas:

- the unity of Word and Sacrament
- the Eucharist as a sacrifice
- the Real Presence of Christ
- continuity and change in the Mass.

Unity of Word and Eucharist

The Mass is in two main parts, the Liturgy of the Word and the Liturgy of the Eucharist. Both the Scriptures and the Body of Christ are given to us to bring us into communion with God. The Scriptures communicate the divine life to us as the Body and Blood of Christ.

In the past, the Liturgy of the Eucharist has tended to be so highly regarded that the Liturgy of the Word has sometimes been undervalued. The Church has, in fact, always venerated the divine Scriptures: think of the jewelled Gospel books and the solemn processions of the Gospel book. By comparison, how often do people read from missalettes, photocopies or bits of paper today, and show little reverence for the lectern? Nonetheless, a new appreciation of the Liturgy of the Word was a fruit of the Second Vatican Council, and it is a point upon which we can focus in our catechesis.

4 How do we show respect for the lectern, the readings and the Gospel?

The Liturgy of the Word and the Liturgy of the Eucharist are intimately related.

The Sacrifice of the Mass

The Mass is not just a 'Church service', an act of worship devised by the Church. It is, first and foremost, a Sacred Mystery given to us by Christ. In the Mass the sacrifice that Jesus completed on Calvary becomes present for us as we re-enact the events of the Last Supper. In the Mass the table of the Last Supper becomes an altar for Christ's sacrifice. Jesus in the Last Supper offers himself in sacrifice 'so that sins may be forgiven'. He is the lamb of sacrifice 'who takes away the sins of the world'. At the heart of this sacrifice is love.

The Mass, then, is a sacrifice because it makes present the sacrifice of the Cross, applying the redemptive fruits of that sacrifice to those present. In the Eucharistic sacrifice the priest, at the altar, stands in the place of Christ, the great High Priest: he acts 'in the person of Christ'. In the Mass we are led to the heart of the mystery through appreciating the sacrificial nature of what is happening.

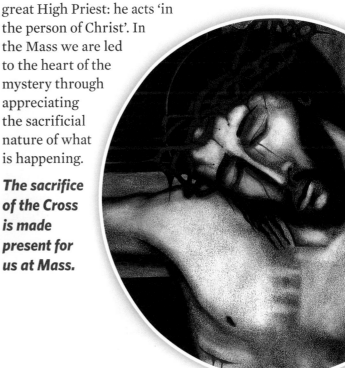

The sacrifice of the Cross is made present for us at Mass.

The Real Presence of Christ

At the heart of the Eucharistic prayer of the Mass are the words of Jesus at the Last Supper transforming the bread and wine into his own body and blood. 'This is my Body... This is the Cup of my Blood'. The Catholic Faith has always held that at the Consecration the bread and wine become Christ's Body and Blood so that only the appearances of bread and wine remain. On the altar, after the consecration, Christ the Lord is present. This is why kneeling in worship and adoration of the Sacred Host is appropriate.

In the Mass, Christ feeds us with himself, not just signs or symbols of himself.

Continuity and Change

The essentials of the Mass cannot change. The liturgy of the Word reflects the Jewish synagogue service that Christ would have attended and the Liturgy of the Eucharist is built around the four key actions of Jesus at the Last Supper: 'taking', 'blessing', 'breaking' and 'giving'.

Blessed Pope John Paul II spoke of the sacred character of the Eucharist in the following way:

'Beginning with the Upper Room and Holy Thursday, the celebration of the Eucharist has a long history, a history as long as that of the Church. In the course of this history, the secondary elements have undergone certain changes, but there has been no change in the essence of the "Mysterium" instituted by the Redeemer of the world at the Last Supper'. (*Dominicae cenae* 8)

Given all the changes in the liturgy that many have experienced, it is important to stress the central, unchanging elements. It is also important to highlight the need to respect the use of approved liturgical texts in all sacramental celebrations, since it is not only the local parish that is praying in isolation – every parish prays as part of the 'whole Christ'.

The essentials of the Mass are unchanging.

Summary

In this session we have looked at:

- **The meaning of 'mystery'.**
- **The mystery of the Eucharist at the centre of the faith.**
- **How to foster an awareness of the mystery in our catechesis.**
- **Overcoming misunderstandings of the Eucharist.**

Further Reading

- CCC 1076-1109: the Holy Trinity at work in the Eucharist and in the liturgy in general.
- CCC 1145-1162: the importance of signs and symbols for revealing the mystery to us in the liturgy.
- CCC 1179-1186; SC 7, 122-127: the symbolism connected with some of the furnishings in a church.
- CCC 1356-1390: the doctrines of the Eucharistic Sacrifice, the Real Presence and Holy Communion.
- Second Vatican Council: *Dei Verbum* 21: on the veneration due to the one 'table' of the Word of God and Body of Christ.

Glossary on the mystery of the Eucharist

Infinite: *without limits. God is infinite. We are the opposite, 'finite', limited.*

Dominicae cenae: *the Apostolic Letter issued by Blessed Pope John Paul II on the Mystery and Worship of the Eucharist in 1980.*

Sacrament: *an outward and visible sign of an inward and invisible grace, instituted by Christ for our salvation.*

Closing Prayer

Lord Jesus Christ,
You gave us the Eucharist as the memorial of your suffering and death. May our worship of this Sacrament of your Body and Blood, help us to experience the salvation won for us, and the peace of the kingdom where you live with the Father and the Holy Spirit, One God, for ever and ever. Amen.

Session 10

'What can we do?'

'Do whatever he tells you' (Jn 2:5)

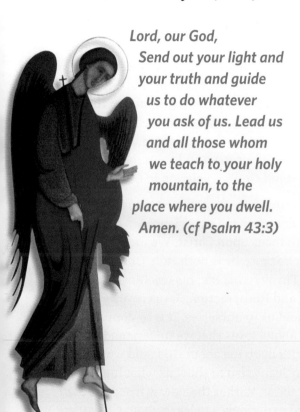

*Lord, our God,
Send out your light and
your truth and guide
us to do whatever
you ask of us. Lead us
and all those whom
we teach to your holy
mountain, to the
place where you dwell.
Amen. (cf Psalm 43:3)*

**In this session we are going to focus
upon God's way of teaching, a way
which has been revealed in Christ.
We shall see what implications this
has for how we can catechise or help.
Then we will look at the structure and
'ingredients' of a catechetical session.
We will be asking what guidance we
can discover from the Church about
what could be in a catechetical session,
irrespective of the subject, age group or
circumstances of those we are teaching.**

A double faithfulness

In our catechetical work we practise a double faithfulness:

• to God and the message he has given
• to the human person, the hearer who is to receive the message.

We must hand on the full message we have been given, without any dilution or mutilation. John Paul II says: 'the person who becomes a disciple of Christ has the right to receive "the word of faith" not in mutilated, falsified or diminished form but whole and entire, in all its rigour and vigour.' (CT 30)

We must hand on the full, undiluted message of Christ in a manner which is appropriate for the particular people to whom we are speaking. The *General Directory for Catechesis* tells us that good catechesis consists in that which enables 'the communication of the whole word of God in the concrete existence of people' (GDC 146).

It is important to remember that human differences should not affect the essential content to be transmitted but only the manner of teaching or transmitting. For example, the reality of the Eucharist is the same for children and for adults, for all nationalities and races, for rich and for poor. *How* one teaches about the Eucharist needs to be different for different audiences, the essence of the teaching must be the same.

Blessed Pope John Paul II sums up these points when he speaks about the methods we use to communicate the faith, 'the method chosen must ultimately be referred to a law that is fundamental for the whole of the Church's life: the law of fidelity to God and of fidelity to man in a single loving attitude' (CT55).

In catechesis we practise a double fidelity: to God and to the human person.

1 **Think about the question of fidelity to God in our teaching. When is this difficult? How do we manage it?**

The Pedagogy of God

God has his own way of teaching, a way that is faithful to who he is and to the human person. God practises the double faithfulness about which we have been speaking. The Church calls God's own teaching methods 'the pedagogy of God'.

(41)

'Pedagogy' means 'way of teaching' and God has his own ways of teaching about himself, of reaching and revealing himself to people's hearts and minds. The fullest expression of God's pedagogy is found in the sending of the Son.

God's method of teaching about himself, then, is *personal*. He does not choose firstly a written text, or an object, but a *person* for the fullest revelation of himself to us. This is God's pedagogy and it has implications for us as catechisers, for we can imitate God in his methods. We can follow God's ways, which are revealed in Christ.

The *General Directory for Catechesis* helps us to see what this entails, and especially the **focus upon conversion** in Christ's teaching.

Jesus taught to bring about conversion and so in our catechesis we need to bear the person's salvation in mind and not be content merely with communicating facts or hoping to give a good experience. The whole world needs to 'hear the summons to salvation, so that through hearing it may believe, through belief it may hope, through hope it may come to love' (DV 1). The attitude of the catechist, therefore, should mirror that of Christ who received people 'as persons loved and sought out by God' (GDC 140).

We cannot escape this continual reference in the Church's documents to catechesis being for the sake of conversion. This does not mean that any pressure for conversion need come from us; God will speak to the person's conscience. But our manner of speaking, our attitudes and what we say can help prepare a person to welcome the action of the Holy Spirit in his or her life. And so we need to consider the way we think, act and speak, the way we encourage, the way we relate what we teach to happiness, to courage, to suffering, to decision making and to joy.

God has a unique way of teaching which we can follow.

Christ and our human experience

We have seen that God the Father teaches by sending his Son, Jesus. In the mystery of the Incarnation God united himself to every human person who has ever existed or will exist – to every one of us – by taking on human nature and living a fully human life.

By doing this, God the Son has not only revealed who *God* is to us, he has also revealed who we are, what a fully human life is. Here is a wonderful quotation from the Second Vatican Council explaining this, a quotation that has been repeated more than any other from the Council by Blessed Pope John Paul II:

'In reality it is only in the mystery of the Word made flesh that the mystery of man truly becomes clear' (GS22).

There has been considerable debate about whether one should begin one's sessions from 'God's side', proclaiming and explaining the truths of Revelation contained in the deposit of faith, or whether one should begin from our own experiences, with what is familiar to us and from there try to understand God's revelation in Christ.

The Church asks us not to oppose these two – doctrine and experience (cf. CT22) – but to **focus upon Christ**. We focus upon Christ because he is both fully God and fully man. Through his life, his teaching and his death and Resurrection, Jesus reveals God to us and us to ourselves. It is by coming to know about Jesus that we understand the Church's doctrine about God, and we can look to Jesus also to show us what human life is about. Rather than draw from our own limited experiences to learn about Christ, we can turn to Christ who wants to give us an experience of himself and his Redemption.

❷ Let us consider two examples from the Gospels: Matthew 9:20-22 and 14:22-33. How does Christ reveal God to us and us to ourselves?

We can make sure our catechesis is centred on Christ who reveals God to us and us to ourselves.

Basic structure for a catechetical session

In *Echoes*, we have considered a number of attitudes and fundamental methodological principles. Now let us draw together what we have examined here and in previous sessions to see what guidance this gives for the structure and content of catechetical sessions.

What does a catechetical session need to contain in order to be faithful to God and to the person and to follow God's own pedagogy which is re-vealed in Christ? Here are some points to consider:

- **Catechesis is above all the work of the Trinity**
It makes sense, therefore, always to start with a way of acknowledging the presence of the Trinity. This could be a time of quiet, or of prayer, or it could mean opening with a hymn or a short meditative reading from Scripture.

- **Catechesis hands on what God has chosen to reveal of himself and his plan of love.** It makes sense, therefore, to select systematically from the deposit of faith entrusted to the Church. Here we have all that God has revealed of himself and his plan. We turn to Scripture, to the Catechism, to the great Doctors and Councils of the Church and to the writing of the Popes.

- **Catechesis needs to give people knowledge of the story of salvation.** All teaching should be linked into the Story of Salvation in some way. This is the Catholic story which we invite our hearers to understand as their Story, too.

- **Catechesis brings people into communion with Christ.** It makes sense, therefore, to have various activities to help people link their lives and experiences with the life of Jesus so that they can understand how the grace of God in Christ can change our lives, filling us with faith, hope and love.

- **Catechesis always aims at conversion of the person.** God created us out of love, and has revealed his merciful plan to redeem us from sin and death in order to bring us to share in the eternal joy of the Trinity. Our catechesis is therefore always aimed at highlighting God's saving work, offered to us in Christ. Our catechesis will include clear ways to respond to the gracious invitation of God so that his image might be restored in us.

- **Catechesis brings us to the liturgy where we receive Christ and join our lives to him.** It is good to always link our catechesis to the liturgy in some way and conclude our sessions with a form of worship. This might be a simple prayer of thanksgiving for whatever has taken place, acknowledging the work of the Trinity, or the session might lead into Benediction or into a Mass. We invite those whom we are catechising into worship of the One they recognise and claim as their Lord.

So, we can sum up the elements we have been considering as:

- Being rooted in the presence of God
- Communicating the deposit of faith
- Telling the Story
- Relating to Christ
- Seeking Conversion
- Linking to liturgy and worship

These elements can be present in every catechetical session.

All catechetical sessions will contain certain ingredients in order to be faithful to God and to the person.

3 Think of a catechetical session in which you were involved. Which of the elements which we have looked at were included? How might you have included the other elements?

Summary

In this session we have looked at:

- **the double fidelity we are called to practise: to God and to the human person.**
- **God's unique way of teaching which we can follow.**
- **the importance of centring our catechesis on Christ who reveals God to us and us to ourselves.**
- **some key components of a catechetical session.**

Further Reading

- On the pedagogy of God: GDC 139-147.
- On doctrine, experience and the centrality of Christ: CCC 425-429 and CT 5-9, 22.

Glossary on Pedagogy

Pedagogy: *way of teaching, especially referring to children. The pedagogy of God, is God's way of teaching us as his own children.*

Methodology: *a system of ways of doing, teaching or studying something.*

Methodological principles: *principles are starting points. Every one has them whether they realise it or not. Typical examples would be 'above all keep them quiet', or 'the main thing is to keep them happy'. These are principles or starting points that guide the methods people choose. The Church asks our starting point to be the double fidelity we looked at.*

Final Prayer

Our Father,
Who art in Heaven,
Hallowed be thy name.
Thy kingdom come,
Thy will be done,
On earth as it is in heaven.
Give us this day our daily bread
And forgive us our trespasses
As we forgive those who trespass against us.
And lead us not into temptation
But deliver us from evil.
Amen.

Session 11

What next?

'Put out into the deep!' (Lk 5:4)

Lord Jesus, we put our trust in you and step out to you in faith. May we always keep our gaze fixed on you, knowing that you are the Lord of all things, and that in our time of need you will always stretch out your hand to save us and bring us your peace. Amen

In this final session we have a sense of both a finishing and a beginning. We are finishing this short series but we are also looking forward to what needs to be done for Christ and his Church, what needs to be done to make the infinite mercy and love of God real for those around us. The Church says that catechesis is intimately connected to evangelisation. We will look at what this means and at the call to us to be evangelisers, as well as to take our continuing development in faith, hope and love seriously.

We have opened this final session with a quotation from the Gospel of St Luke. Blessed Pope John Paul II, in his Apostolic Letter for the new millennium, *Novo Millennio ineunte* (NMI), uses this phrase to sum up what Christ is asking of his Church. We are to 'put out into the deep'. As we do so, says Blessed Pope John Paul II, we can 'remember the past with gratitude... live the present with enthusiasm and ...look forward to the future with confidence' because 'Jesus Christ is the same yesterday and today and for ever' (Heb 13:8). The Lord is always with us, to the end of time.

1 **Let us read the account of the episode from St Luke from which the quotation comes. (Luke 5:1-11)**

The deep of the Good News

What is the deep into which we are to entrust ourselves? The *good news of God* has never-ending depths. God sent his whole Word, plan and desire in his Son, to show and tell mankind, finally and definitively, everything he wanted people to know about himself, about themselves and about ultimate happiness. The Church uses the word evangelisation for the depths and extent of passing on this good news. Are we convinced of this good news ourselves in order to be able to help others to know it?

The document on evangelisation, *Evangelii nuntiandi*, explains to us the content of the good news that we have to offer:

> 'Evangelisation will always contain, as the foundation, the centre and the apex of its whole dynamic power, this explicit declaration: in Jesus Christ who became man, died and rose again from the dead, salvation is offered to every man as the gift of the grace and mercy of God himself.'
> (see Lk 4:22; EN 27)

The Church recognises **three stages of evangelisation** – that is, of discovering and offering to others God's good news:

- The first is called **initial proclamation** – if no one hears the good news very simply they will never know what it is about.
- The second stage is called **catechesis**. Once people have heard the good news and have responded to Christ in faith, they want to learn much more.

- The third stage is **on-going formation**. This is the desire to go deeper and deeper into the good news because it has been found as the pearl of great price, the only thing that satisfies us to the depths of our being. The Church encourages us to think in terms of a lifelong learning of the Faith.

Jesus Christ and the salvation he brings is the heart of the good news, good news with unfathomable depths about which we can discover more and more.

The deep of the person

Catechesis, then, is a vital part of the great process of evangelization, making God's good news known, loved and lived. A lack of **initial proclamation** which really touches a person deeply hinders the desire for catechesis. Without **catechesis** there is no deepening of the message, no development of life 'in Christ', no growth in understanding of that which matters more to living than anything else. A lack of **on-going formation** hinders adult life because a superficial knowledge of the Faith cannot sustain one in the deep complexities of adult experience.

We need to participate in all three stages of evangelization. We need to do so for the sake of our Christian growth and because God and his plan of love for the world is that which is most rewarding to learn about.

2 **Each person needs to be evangelized throughout his or her lifetime.**

New evangelisation

For many in the Western world catechesis has taken place without any significant desire for it, or conversion to Christ accompanying it. People know about Jesus but this has not deeply affected their lives. The Holy Father speaks of the need for 'a new evangelisation' for such people:

'Frequently, many who come for catechesis truly require genuine conversion. Only by starting with conversion can catechesis, strictly speaking, fulfil its proper task of education in the faith'. (GDC 62; CT 19)

In fact, it cannot be assumed that *initial proclamation, catechesis,* and *ongoing formation* have taken place in that order at all.

It is good to avoid the danger of thinking that a particular 'stage' in evangelisation is complete and finished with, or that the majority of the people in our churches are simply in the process of maturing in faith. This may not be the case at all. There are likely to be significant and important elements missing in most people's journey of faith, and elements in need of reawakening and renewal.

3 **What implications might there be here for catechesis in your parish?**

In our catechesis we need to bear in mind the need to give initial proclamation as well.

The deep of the world

The opening quotation from the Gospel of St Luke suggests that the apostles are to go deep into *the world* to 'pay out their nets for a catch'. St Luke records Jesus' teaching in the Parable of the Sower (Mk 4:3-8) which explains what the world is like. In this parable Jesus describes the world in terms of different types of soil in which the seed of the Word of God is sown.

'Today, Jesus Christ, present in the Church through his Spirit, continues to scatter the Word of the Father ever more widely in the field of the world. The conditions of the soil into which it falls vary greatly.' (GDC 15)

The Parable of the Sower speaks of the hard path, the rocky soil, the choked soil and finally the good, fruitful soil. The world into which we echo the Word of God has the same mix of soils, some receptive and welcoming; some indifferent and some hostile to the seed. In his encyclical letter on catechesis, Blessed Pope John Paul II wrote this about the less promising soils:

'Christians today must be formed to live in a world which largely ignores God... To "hold on" in this world, to offer to all a "dialogue of salvation" in which each person feels respected in his or her most basic dignity, the dignity of one who is seeking God, we need a catechesis which trains the young people and adults of our communities to remain clear and consistent in their faith, to affirm serenely their Christian and Catholic identity, to "see Him who is invisible", and to adhere so firmly to the absoluteness of God that they can be witnesses to him in a materialistic civilization that denies Him.' (CT 57)

Whatever the soil, we are still faced with the identical task: to bear witness, simply and clearly, to God as he is revealed by the Lord Jesus Christ. We bring the Good News to all. The *General Directory for Catechesis* asks us to bear the 'field' in mind in a spirit of 'faith and mercy'. We are to look upon the field as God does, with his merciful eyes, longing for the salvation of all.

We can go deep into the world because the world has this depth. We know that every person has been created by God and for God and can find happiness only in a life with him. As St Thomas Aquinas said, 'God alone satisfies'. If we put out our nets in this deep, bearing clear witness to this truth, we will be amazed at our catch.

Echoing Christ today involves bearing witness to him in a spirit of faith and mercy, in a world where many doubt, deny or ignore him.

The deep of prayer

Blessed Pope John Paul II describes the deep as *prayer*, as our communion with Christ. When we pray we swim, as it were, out of our depth and learn to rely on Christ. And it is when we are united to Christ in the deep of prayer that we will make our catch. There is a call here, then, to make our relationship with Christ our priority. Our work in catechesis depends upon this.

Prayer roots us in the truth that our lives and work depend upon Christ.

Go forward in hope!

Blessed Pope John Paul II concludes his Letter for the new millennium by saying that the future opens before the Church 'like a vast ocean upon which we shall venture, relying on the help of Christ. The Son of God, who became incarnate two thousand years ago out of love for humanity, is at work even today: we need discerning eyes to see this,

and above all, a generous heart to become the instruments of his work.' (NMI 58)

The men and women around us ask believers not only to 'speak' of Christ, but to 'show' him to them as well. We need to witness to Christ with our lives as well as speak about him. Our witness, however, will be hopelessly inadequate if we ourselves have not first *contemplated his face* in prayer. As our footsteps 'travel the highways of the world', says Blessed Pope John Paul II, we must set our gaze ever more firmly on the face of the Lord. (NMI 16, 58)

The *General Directory for Catechesis* concludes with this reflection: 'May patience and trust abide in the spirituality of the catechist, since it is God himself who sows, gives growth, and brings to fruition the seed of his word, planted in good soil and tended with love.'

The effectiveness of catechesis, says the Directory, is a work of grace, 'is and always will be a gift of God, through the operation of the Spirit of the Father and the Son.' The authors of the Directory remind us of St. Paul who, in his first letter to the Corinthians, confirms this total dependence on grace, the work of God: 'I planted, Apollos watered, but God gave the growth. So neither he who plants, nor he who waters is anything, but only God who gives the growth' (1 Cor 3: 6-7). (see GDC 288-9)

Summary

In this final session we have considered:

- **Blessed Pope John Paul II's call to 'put out into the deep'.**
- **The variety of conditions of the people we meet.**
- **Being sure that we know in our minds and our hearts what is the 'good news' which we are offering.**
- **The three stages of deepening the faith and the need for our catechesis to link to initial proclamation and to on-going formation.**

Further reading

- For the three stages of evangelisation and their relationship to each other: GDC 60-72.
- For the need to root ourselves in prayer: CCC 2559-2565; NMI 32-34.

Glossary on evangelisation

Evangelisation: *proclaiming the good news of Jesus Christ who has revealed the mystery of God and his plan of love. It comes from two Greek words, 'eu' meaning 'good' and 'angelion' meaning message ('angelos' or 'angel' means messenger).*

Gospel: *'Gospel' comes from two Anglo-Saxon words, 'god' meaning 'good' and 'spell' meaning 'speech' or 'message'. Gospel, then, also means 'good news'. Four evangelists wrote the four Gospels. That is, four messengers of good news wrote four accounts of good news.*

New evangelisation: *where the baptised have lost a living sense of faith, or even no longer consider themselves members of the Church and live a life far removed from Christ and his Gospel. Such situations require a new evangelisation (cf. GDC 586).*

The new situation is the situation of people who may have had to study Christianity, such as in school, but for whom no depth in the message has been grasped and no depth in the person has been reached.

Initial proclamation: *the first proclamation of the Catholic faith, giving the centre and heart of the good news.*

Formation: *the development of the whole person in Christ.*

On-going formation: *a continuing exploration of the fathomless riches of God's revelation.*

Final meditation and prayer

'Indeed we also work, but we are only collaborating with God who works, for his mercy has gone before us. It has gone before us so that we may be healed, and follows us so that once healed, we may be given life; it goes before us so that we may be called, and follows us so that we may be glorified; it goes before us so that we may live devoutly, and follows us so that we may always live with God: for without him we can do nothing.'

(St Augustine of Hippo)

God our Father,
We praise you that you have made us for yourself. You have given us life that we may come to know you, the fullness of our joy and the end of all our desires. We place your Church under the protection of Mary our Mother, St Joseph, St Michael, the angels and all the saints. As we go forward in hope, continue to fill us with your grace so that we may speak of you and your truth, goodness and beauty, and witness to you with our lives. We ask this in the power of your Spirit and in the name of your Son, who is our Way, our Truth and our Life. Amen.